American Civil War 1861–65

Union Sharpshooter

VERSUS

Confederate Sharpshooter

Gary Yee

Illustrated by Johnny Shumate

OSPREY PUBLISHING
Bloomsbury Publishing Plc
PO Box 883, Oxford, OX1 9PL, UK
1385 Broadway, 5th Floor, New York, NY 10018, USA
E-mail: info@ospreypublishing.com
www.ospreypublishing.com

OSPREY is a trademark of Osprey Publishing Ltd

First published in Great Britain in 2019

A catalog record for this book is available from the British Library.

ISBN: PB 9781472831859; eBook 9781472832122;
ePDF 9781472832115; XML 9781472832108

19 20 21 22 23   10 9 8 7 6 5 4 3 2 1

Maps by bounford.com
Index by Rob Munro
Typeset by PDQ Digital Media Solutions, Bungay, UK
Printed in China through World Print Ltd.

Osprey Publishing supports the Woodland Trust, the UK's leading
woodland conservation charity.

To find out more about our authors and books visit www.
ospreypublishing.com. Here you will find extracts, author interviews,
details of forthcoming events and the option to sign up for our
newsletter.

Dedication

This book is dedicated to my uncle, Bill Yee, who introduced me to
firearms.

Acknowledgments

The author gratefully acknowledges the assistance of Company of
Military Historians' Bill Adams for his insights and expertise in firearms
and accoutrements; 45th Infantry Division Museum Curator Mike
Gonzales; Fredericksburg and Spotsylvania National Military Park Chief
Historian Ranger John Hennessy; West Point Army Museum Curator Les
Jensen; Tom Lunt; Martin Pegler; Alan Sissenwein; Bob Velke; National
Firearms Museum Curator Doug Wicklund; my editor, Nick Reynolds,
who saw this book through from inception to publication; and the
illustrator, Johnny Shumate.

Key to military symbols

Army Group	Army	Corps
Division	Brigade	Regiment
Battalion	Company/Battery	Platoon
Section	Squad	Infantry
Artillery	Cavalry	Airborne
Unit HQ	Air defence	Air Force
Air mobile	Air transportable	Amphibious
Anti-tank	Armour	Air aviation
Bridging	Engineer	Headquarters
Maintenance	Medical	Missile
Mountain	Navy	Nuclear, biological, chemical
Ordnance	Parachute	Reconnaissance
Signal	Supply	Transport movement
Fortress or static	Fortress machine gun	

Key to unit identification

Unit identifier — Parent unit
Commander
(+) with added elements
(−) less elements

CONTENTS

INTRODUCTION   4

THE OPPOSING SIDES   8
Origins • Recruitment and training • Sharpshooter roles and tactics • Leadership and communications

FREDERICKSBURG   33
December 11–15, 1862

VICKSBURG   47
May 18–July 4, 1863

BATTERY WAGNER   59
July 19–September 6, 1863

ANALYSIS   73
Fredericksburg • Vicksburg • Battery Wagner

AFTERMATH   76

SELECT BIBLIOGRAPHY   78

INDEX   80

Introduction

After Fort Sumter in Charleston Harbor was fired upon on April 12, 1861, Americans on both sides of the Mason–Dixon Line were whipped into a war frenzy. Young men of all occupations and backgrounds rushed to enlist, some to defend the Union and the honor of the flag and others to defend their rights by seceding from it.

Since the American Revolutionary War (1775–83), American military theory had been based on European models, but was little influenced by the adoption of the Minié ball in 1855. Two European schools of thought on the battlefield use of long-range rifles emerged before 1861. The Belgian school of thought believed that firing would commence at 1,000yd and combatants would approach no closer than 600yd, it being too dangerous to move any closer. The other was the Prussian School, whose adherents also believed

Perhaps the most famous sharpshooter of the era, Hiram Berdan raised two regiments of marksmen for the Union. Each candidate demonstrated his skill by placing ten consecutive shots in a 10in circle at 200yd. In this illustration from *Frank Leslie's Illustrated Almanac*, Berdan's sharpshooters are shown in trench defenses at Washington, DC, exhibiting their skills to Major General George B. McClellan and his staff. (Buyenlarge/Getty Images)

These Union gunners are pictured with 13in seacoast mortars during the siege of Yorktown (April 5–May 4, 1862). The artillerymen of both sides would quickly learn to fear the long-range, accurate fire of the sharpshooters during the sieges of the Civil War. In response to the tactical superiority asserted by the Union sharpshooters over the Confederates at Yorktown, the Confederates would raise their own units of sharpshooters. (Library of Congress)

firing would commence at long distance, but that close-order combat was still viable. For many Americans, the matter was settled by the French and Sardinian victory over Austria at the battle of Solferino on June 24, 1859, during the Second War of Italian Independence. It came to be believed that an exchange of fire would precede use of the bayonet, which would then decide the battle; the advantages conferred by long-range shooting were dismissed.

Amid the many regiments entering Union service were numerous newly raised sharpshooter units. Many of their officers came from a nonmilitary background, however, and even the graduates from military academies among them were ignorant of the sharpshooters' potential. Only a handful of officers initially recognized the value of marksmen who could serve as skilled skirmishers or as long-range marksmen capable of countering the enemy's sharpshooters.

By contrast the Confederacy did not raise sharpshooters at first, confident of its men's innate superiority in terms of marksmanship. In the years before 1861 several Southern militia companies called themselves sharpshooters, but such titles were honorific and did not reflect such units' skills or equipment. Traditionally, the "flank companies" of each regiment could be called upon to perform a sharpshooting role. Certainly, there was no shortage of competent marksmen in the Confederacy, but very few had experience with the longer-range Minié longarms used by the US military after 1855. Minié weapons were unavailable to the antebellum hunter and the only US factories which produced Minié longarms (Harper's Ferry in Virginia and Springfield Armory in Massachusetts) made them for the military. Even if a Confederate soldier managed to acquire a Springfield rifle-musket, he needed to familiarize himself with its ballistics. Poor distance estimation or failing to adjust one's sight either resulted in the Minié ball overshooting or falling short of its target.

Two types of sharpshooters would fight in the Civil War. One was the infantryman who fought as a specialized skirmisher, while the other was the target rifle-equipped sharpshooter who in functional terms was more akin to today's sniper. The concept of how to use a sharpshooter armed with a specialized long-range rifle was understood neither by the professional, academy-trained officer nor by most of his civilian volunteer officer

MAP KEY

While the major effort of the Civil War centered upon Virginia and the successful defense or capture of the Confederate capitol of Richmond, no state that became part of the Confederacy was spared from the conflict.

The first of the three clashes examined in this study was fought at Fredericksburg, Virginia, during December 11–15, 1862. While Fredericksburg has long been known as the Civil War battlefield where Union soldiers threw themselves futilely against Confederate troops protected by the stone wall at Marye's Heights, the river crossing attempted by the Union forces at the outset of the battle is largely overlooked. It was among the first battles in which sharpshooting played a key role in making a Confederate victory possible.

The second clash is the Union siege of Confederate-held Vicksburg, Mississippi (May 18–July 4, 1863). Major General Ulysses S. Grant crossed the Mississippi River and after marching south past Vicksburg, rendezvoused with Rear Admiral David D. Porter's Union Navy fleet and landed near Bruinsburg, Mississippi.

From there Grant fought five battles, marching back and forth and defeating each successive Confederate army thrown in his path. After 17 days, his army stood outside the heights that guarded Vicksburg. Two attempts to storm the heights and capture Vicksburg by *coup de main* failed; unwilling to risk another assault, Grant settled down for a siege. This provided ideal conditions for sharpshooting in which the Union would soon gain the upper hand.

The final clash examined took place near South Carolina's seaport town of Charleston. Known to both belligerents as the hotbed of secession, Charleston witnessed the shots that started the Civil War. From Charleston blockade-runners could sortie with loads of cotton and return with scarce items needed by the Confederacy. Charleston was also the terminus of rail lines which connected the town to Savannah and to the interior. The siege of Battery Wagner (July 19–September 6, 1863), in which a Union force besieged the Confederate defenders of Morris Island near Charleston, would involve sharpshooting as important and contentious as that conducted during World War I.

counterparts. The sharpshooters' potential would slowly be realized as the school of the battlefield forced the understanding upon them. The greater availability of repeating and breechloading rifles in the North initially gave the Union sharpshooters a firepower advantage over their Confederate counterparts. Additionally, the Union had more target rifles fitted with telescopic sights in the early part of the war – notably during the siege of Yorktown (April 5–May 4, 1862) – which gave them an advantage of range. The Confederates would not start to draw level until Whitworth rifles began arriving in the Confederacy in 1863.

Although a poor-quality image, this is a rare contemporary photograph of a Confederate sharpshooter. He would be almost impossible to see in heavy undergrowth or foliage. While difficult to discern, this Confederate sharpshooter wields a heavy-barrel target rifle. Besides the Whitworth and the Kerr, domestically manufactured firearms intended for sharpshooters and scouts were made or assembled by the Confederate arsenal in Macon, Georgia. They also had quite a number of spare telescopes awaiting rifles to be affixed to. Additionally, there were numerous private gunsmiths who were capable of making target rifles like their northern brethren. (Martin Pegler)

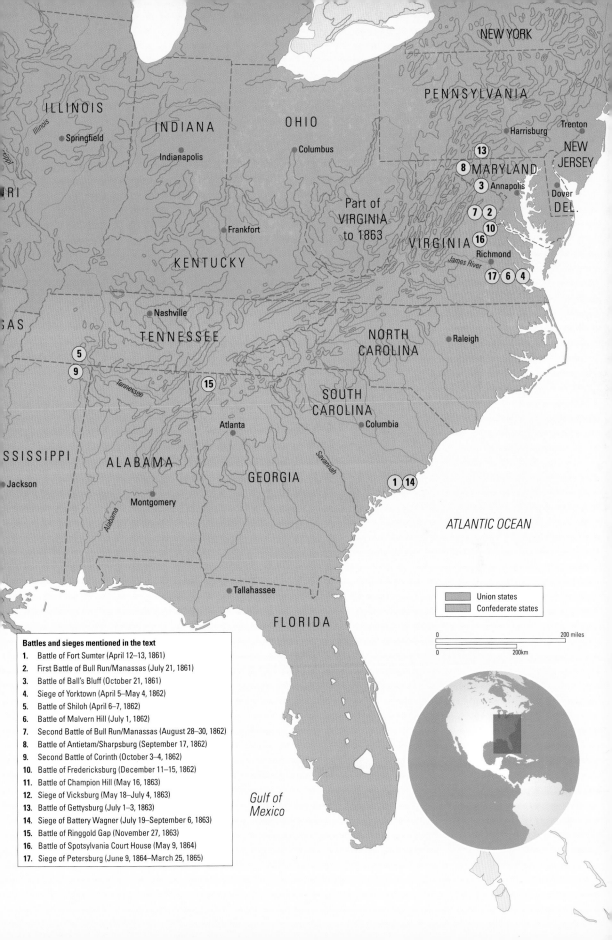

NEW YORK

PENNSYLVANIA

ILLINOIS

INDIANA

OHIO

Springfield

Indianapolis

Columbus

Harrisburg

Trenton

NEW JERSEY

13

8 MARYLAND

3 Annapolis

Dover

DEL.

Part of
VIRGINIA
to 1863

7 **2**

10

16

VIRGINIA

Richmond

Frankfort

KENTUCKY

James River

17 **6** **4**

Nashville

TENNESSEE

NORTH
CAROLINA

Raleigh

5

9

Tennessee

15

SOUTH
CAROLINA

Columbia

SSISSIPPI

ALABAMA

Atlanta

GEORGIA

Savannah

Jackson

Montgomery

Alabama

1 **14**

ATLANTIC OCEAN

Tallahassee

FLORIDA

Union states
Confederate states

0   200 miles
0   200km

Gulf of
Mexico

Battles and sieges mentioned in the text

1.   Battle of Fort Sumter (April 12–13, 1861)
2.   First Battle of Bull Run/Manassas (July 21, 1861)
3.   Battle of Ball's Bluff (October 21, 1861)
4.   Siege of Yorktown (April 5–May 4, 1862)
5.   Battle of Shiloh (April 6–7, 1862)
6.   Battle of Malvern Hill (July 1, 1862)
7.   Second Battle of Bull Run/Manassas (August 28–30, 1862)
8.   Battle of Antietam/Sharpsburg (September 17, 1862)
9.   Second Battle of Corinth (October 3–4, 1862)
10. Battle of Fredericksburg (December 11–15, 1862)
11. Battle of Champion Hill (May 16, 1863)
12. Siege of Vicksburg (May 18–July 4, 1863)
13. Battle of Gettysburg (July 1–3, 1863)
14. Siege of Battery Wagner (July 19–September 6, 1863)
15. Battle of Ringgold Gap (November 27, 1863)
16. Battle of Spotsylvania Court House (May 9, 1864)
17. Siege of Petersburg (June 9, 1864–March 25, 1865)

The Opposing Sides

ORIGINS

Union

Among the visionary loyalists eager to put down the Rebellion, Crimean War veteran Casper Trepp championed the concept of an elite unit composed of marksmen who would serve as expert skirmishers and dominate the battlefield. Trepp wrote several newspaper articles calling for the creation of a special corps of sharpshooters and appealed for someone to lobby Washington, DC for its approval, but being a Swiss immigrant, Trepp lacked the political connections required to bring his idea to fruition. Entering the picture was New York engineer, inventor, and celebrated marksman, Hiram Berdan, who sought and received permission from Secretary of War Simon Cameron to raise a regiment of marksmen. So enthusiastic was the response that instead of the envisioned one regiment of marksmen, two were raised and even a third contemplated. (With three regiments, Berdan fancied he would receive his brigadier's star.) Trepp for his part raised the first company, Company A of the 1st United States Sharpshooters (1st USSS), which was composed mostly of Swiss and German immigrants. While short of the 30 companies hoped for by Berdan, 20 companies were raised, but at the last moment, Massachusetts Governor John A. Andrew decided that the two Massachusetts companies should serve exclusively alongside Massachusetts regiments and not as part of Berdan's Sharpshooters. As a result, the 2d USSS was only eight companies strong instead of ten. Governor Andrew believed that besides his state being able to furnish the Massachusetts soldiers with superior arms, their families would receive benefits from the state. The two Massachusetts companies would subsequently be known after their governor as the 1st and 2d Andrew Sharpshooters.

In the Department of the West, its commanding general, Major General John C. Fremont, also decided to raise a regiment of sharpshooters. Drawing

upon men reputed to be the best shots from the Midwestern states, the regiment was organized originally as the 14th Missouri Volunteer Infantry and was mustered into Union service on November 23, 1861. Named after its colonel, John S. Birge, the regiment was known as Birge's Western Sharpshooters and from November 20, 1862 onward was officially known as the 66th Illinois Volunteer Infantry. While the regiment's men were never granted sharpshooter status by the War Department, it was understood by their role what they were.

The last regiment-sized unit recognized by the War Department was the 1st Michigan Sharpshooters, raised by Michigan Governor Austin Blair in response to President Abraham Lincoln's 1862 call for more men. The regiment was unique in that its men received marksmanship training in order to qualify as sharpshooters. Six companies were mustered on July 7, 1863, and the regiment's first assignment was chasing down Confederate raider Brigadier General John H. Morgan. Other units captured Morgan and in August the 1st Michigan Sharpshooters reported to Camp Douglas, Illinois, where the men of the regiment served as guards for Confederate prisoners. The regiment later fought in the Army of the Potomac.

One Union regiment that was supposed to have been sharpshooters was the 203d Pennsylvania Volunteer Infantry. Clad in surplus green uniforms originally made for Berdan's Sharpshooters, the men of the 203d were promised .56-56 Spencer lever-action repeating rifles but were armed with Springfield rifle-muskets instead. Furthermore, no evidence has been found to show that the men satisfied the War Department's sharpshooter qualification. Consequently, they were used as regular infantry and did not fight as sharpshooters.

Besides the various regiments, there were several battalion- and company-sized sharpshooter units. Six companies strong, the 1st Maine Sharpshooters never received recognition as a sharpshooter battalion and served in the 3d Brigade, 1st Division of Major General Gouverneur K. Warren's V Corps. The battalion was disbanded on June 21, 1865, its men ordered into the 20th Maine Volunteer Infantry. Ohio raised ten companies of which the first three became part of the multi-state Birge's Western Sharpshooters. The 4th Company was attached to the 79th Ohio Volunteer Infantry; the 5th, 6th, 7th, and 8th companies were formed into a battalion led by Captain Gershom M. Barber; the 9th Company was attached to the 16th Ohio Volunteer Infantry; and the 10th Company was attached to the 60th Ohio

In this illustration from *Harper's Weekly*, Hiram Berdan is depicted practicing firing at a target at Weehawken, New Jersey. Interestingly, while Berdan served as a colonel and drew a salary, he was never commissioned as a colonel. (© CORBIS/Corbis via Getty Images)

Perched high in a tree and out of range of the enemy, this Union sharpshooter is aiming his target rifle. Because he is level with his target, he need not calculate for elevation where the line of sight to the target is longer than the actual shorter horizontal distance. He knows that a failure to calculate for the shorter distance in uphill or downhill shooting will cause him to overshoot and miss. Since his rifle does not accept government ammunition, he had to "run" (cast) and size his own bullets and make his own cartridges at camp. This frees him from the awkwardness of using a powder flask and measure in a tree.

Weapons, dress, and equipment

He is armed with a target rifle (**1**) which he privately purchased and used in civilian shooting matches. Like the rifles St. Louis gunsmith Horace Dimick supplied to Birge's Western Sharpshooters, privately made hunting or target rifles saw limited use during the war. A target rifle could have a set trigger, giving it a lighter trigger than almost any government-issued firearm. Such weapons could also have special sights. While not fitted with a telescope – rare but not unknown in the Midwest – this rifle has a rear aperture sight.

Like other Union soldiers in the Army of the Tennessee, this man's unit was late to adopt corps badges and his wool forage cap (**2**) reflects this. His four-button woolen sack coat (**3**) was widely worn throughout the Union Army. He wears sky-blue woolen pants (**4**) and government-issued shoes (**5**) which are in good condition.

Suspended from a shoulder strap with brass eagle plate (**6**), his Pattern 1861 cartridge box (**7**) carries his handmade paper cartridges. The shoulder strap is secured by his waist belt (**8**) with a brass "US" buckle near his cap pouch (**9**). Hanging from a branch and within easy reach behind him are his cloth-covered canteen (**10**) and haversack (**11**).

Hailing from Burlington, Ostego County, New York, Truman Head settled in California, where he hunted grizzlies. Aged 52 in 1861, Head enlisted in Captain Benjamin Duesler's company, later Company C, 1st USSS, and acquired the monikers "California Joe" and "Old Californy." Head's privately acquired Sharps Model 1859 double-trigger breechloading rifle became the envy of the regiment. On April 11, 1862 Head was skirmishing with his Sharps when its band was struck by a Confederate bullet, bending the barrel, shattering the forearm of the stock, and inflicting facial injuries. Head is depicted here with his rifle shortly afterward. Head also used a heavy-barrel target telescope rifle and was witnessed making an 800yd hit. In an April 14, 1862 letter home, Private Thomas H. Mann, serving with the 18th Massachusetts Volunteer Infantry, explained that he had examined Head's rifle; Mann noted that the rifle weighed 32lb and made a point of mentioning the telescope that ran the length of the barrel (Hennessy 2000: 55–56). Failing eyesight caused Head to be hospitalized after Malvern Hill (July 1, 1862). He briefly returned to duty, but was hospitalized again before South Mountain (September 14, 1862) and was discharged on November 3, 1862. Returning to California, Head worked as a night inspector at the San Francisco Customs House for one year before being demoted to laborer there. He died in 1875 and is buried in San Francisco's Presidio Cemetery. (Interim Archives/Getty Images)

Volunteer Infantry. The 1st Battalion New York Volunteer Sharpshooters included the 6th, 7th, 8th, and 9th companies of New York Sharpshooters.

Lastly, there were numerous company-sized units including Brady's Independent Company of Sharpshooters, organized in Detroit, Michigan on February 3, 1862 and attached to the 16th Michigan Volunteer Infantry. They were later reinforced by Jardine's Independent Company of Sharpshooters, organized in Saginaw, Michigan on May 3, 1864 and subsequently absorbed into Brady's Company of Sharpshooters. The 11th Company of the 56th New York Volunteer Infantry was that regiment's sharpshooter company. During the Civil War it was not unusual to see ad hoc units raised within the Union Army, with the most skilled marksmen or skirmishers being gathered together into a unit.

Confederate

Unlike the Union, the Confederacy did not raise sharpshooters at the outbreak of war. Dedicated sharpshooters were thought to be unnecessary; to most soldiers, sharpshooting was considered to be just another onerous task the common infantryman could perform. Besides, the war would be over before they would be needed. In lieu of raising sharpshooters, the Confederates followed the old British practice of relying on the flank companies (designated A and K) as skirmishers. The war's progression had some harsh lessons for the Confederates, however. Calling upon the same companies to serve as skirmishers tended to tire the men. The alternative practice – nominating a few men from each company and sending them forward under an officer who did not know them – was not efficient either, as the men and the officers had not trained as a unit.

During a year of exposure to Union sharpshooting, the Confederates came to appreciate the usefulness and necessity of having their own specialized marksmen. If nothing else, they were needed to counter the Union's sharpshooters. The Confederate Congress enabled legislation mandating that each brigade raise a sharpshooter battalion. This was followed on May 3, 1862, by an order in Richmond by Confederate Adjutant General Samuel Cooper that was distributed to the various Confederate armies. While such battalions were supposed to be at least three companies strong, each brigade was left to its own devices with respect to implementing the order. Many sharpshooter units in the Confederate Army of Tennessee and the Confederate Army of the West were raised by the detachment of companies that were then formed into an independent unit.

Irish-born Patrick R. Cleburne served in the British Army prior to emigrating to the United States, where he worked as an apothecary and was later admitted to the Arkansas Bar. Cleburne raised the first sharpshooters in the Confederacy and used a British musketry manual to train his division in marksmanship. (PhotoQuest/Getty Images)

Predating this effort were the actions of the Army of Tennessee's Major General Patrick R. Cleburne, who on his own initiative began training his division in marksmanship and selecting from among the best men who would form a sharpshooter platoon. Battle experience inspired other Confederates in the Army of Northern Virginia, such as Brigadier General Robert E. Rodes, to raise one sharpshooter company in late 1862. After his promotion to division command on December 13, 1862, Rodes expanded it to one battalion per brigade. Brigadier General William T. Wofford implemented similar measures when he raised the 3d Battalion Georgia Sharpshooters.

While recuperating at Wartrace, Tennessee, in the aftermath of the battle of Shiloh (April 6–7, 1862), Cleburne hit upon the notion that sharpshooters would increase the combat effectiveness of his command. Having served in the ranks of the 41st (Welch) Regiment of Foot, Cleburne was aware of the British Army's riflemen; using his British marksmanship handbook, he directed Major Calhoun Benham to instruct his division. An attorney by training, Benham had no sharpshooting expertise and was easily sidetracked into talking about his adventures in California. When Cleburne learned that Benham's students were not learning anything, he took over instructing himself. Eventually, these trainers went on to instruct the entire division. Among his men, Cleburne raised a small corps of sharpshooters who preceded Adjutant General Cooper's order; these men were later armed with British Whitworth or Kerr target rifles. Cleburne, then, can be called the father of Confederate sharpshooting.

In response to Cooper's order, in the Army of Northern Virginia the 1st Battalion North Carolina Sharpshooters was raised by permanently detaching companies B and E of the 21st North Carolina Volunteer Infantry. They were not to remain General Robert E. Lee's sole sharpshooter battalion, however, and were later joined by the 3d Battalion Georgia Sharpshooters, which was raised by select men within Brigadier General Wofford's Brigade of Major General Lafayette McLaws' Division. The third official battalion in the Army of Northern Virginia was the 23d Alabama Battalion Sharpshooters.

This Confederate sharpshooter sits upright behind a large object (not shown) for protection against any return fire. Like he did when he hunted game as a youth, his left eye is closed to help him focus his dominant eye on his target, who is unaware of his presence. Before seating himself, he adjusted his rear sight for the estimated distance of his target. That was part of his training which was based on the marksmanship manual from the Hythe School of Musketry in Britain. As he steadies his aim and controls his breathing, his finger slowly feels the trigger and begins a rearward pressure until the gun discharges and sends the bullet to the hapless target.

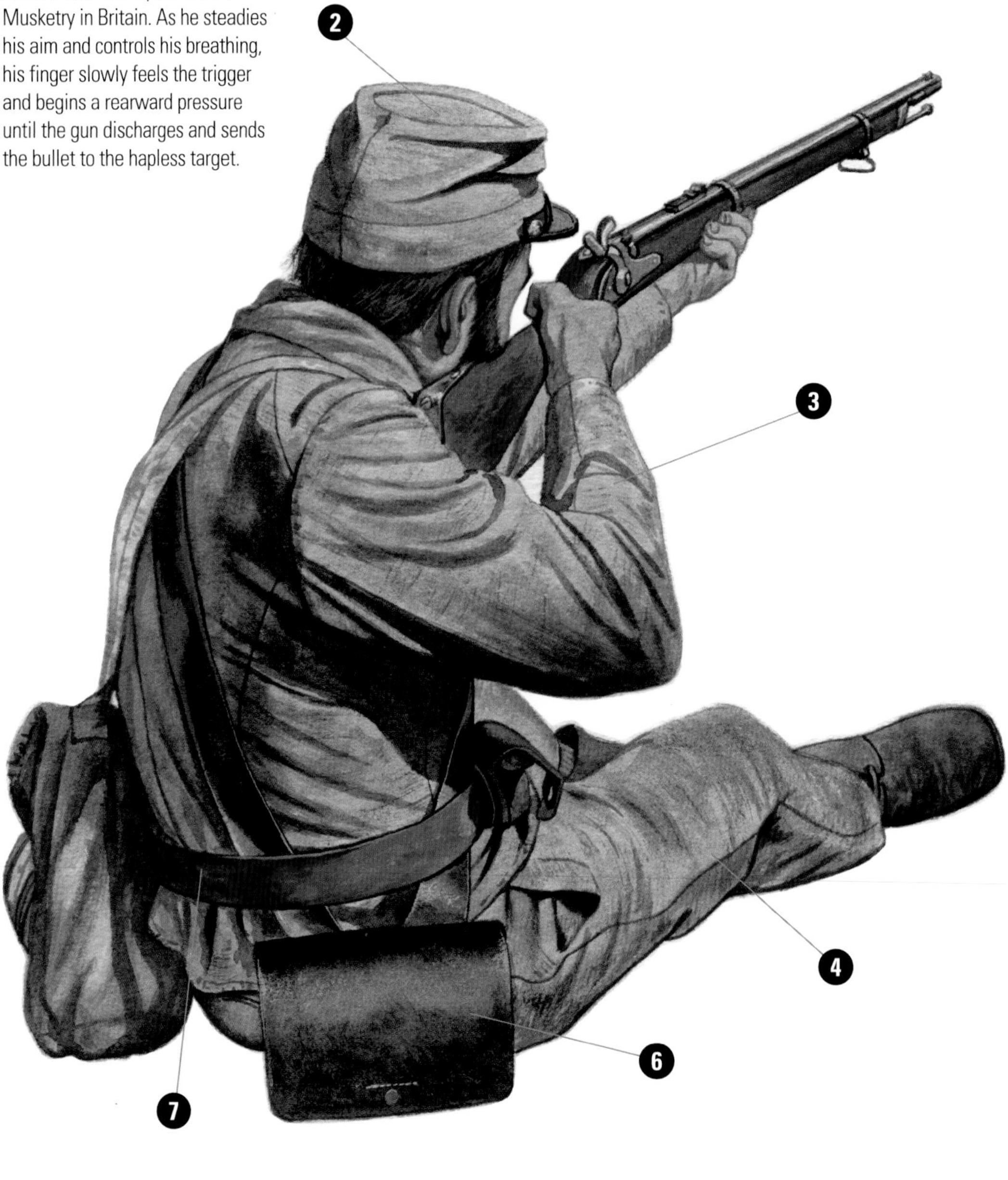

2

3

4

6

7

Weapons, dress, and equipment

He is using a .577-caliber Enfield Pattern 1856 two-band short rifle (**1**) with 33in barrel. The light and handy Pattern 1856s were reserved for the sharpshooter battalions. Confederate tests in both the Army of Northern Virginia and the Army of Tennessee found the Pattern 1856 to be the most accurate of all normal infantry arms and capable of hitting man-sized targets beyond the 500yd range of other infantry arms.

Unlike most Confederates, who wore round hats that provided better protection from the sun, this Confederate sharpshooter wears a kepi (**2**). His gray jacket (**3**) and "butternut" pants (**4**) are in very good shape, as are his shoes (**5**), which were taken from a dead

Union soldier. His Enfield cartridge box (**6**), imported from Britain, is suspended from a shoulder strap secured by his brown waist belt (**7**). Over his right shoulder he carries a haversack (**8**) containing his rations, and a wooden canteen (**9**). While Berdan's men were issued a calfskin linen-lined knapsack, to the exterior of which was attached their messkit, Confederate sharpshooters were much more basically equipped. Sergeant Berry Benson of McGowan's Sharpshooters recalled abandoning his knapsack and grabbing only his blanket before Major General George E. Pickett's defeat at Five Forks on April 1, 1865 (Benson 1992: 195).

Not all brigades in the Army of Northern Virginia complied with Cooper's order. The endless campaigns of 1862 – Seven Days' Battles (June 25–July 1), Second Bull Run/Manassas (August 28–30), Antietam/Sharpsburg (September 17), and Fredericksburg (December 11–15) – as well as the high casualties gave the brigades little opportunity to do so and by 1863, the order had been forgotten. Besides, the Army of Northern Virginia was so successful under Lee that no one was about to raise the issue. It was not until the winter of 1864 that Lee himself issued an order to raise sharpshooters. More often than not Lee's Army of Northern Virginia relied on ad hoc battalions which were raised by detaching men from their parent regiment and temporarily assigning them to the sharpshooter battalion within their brigade. At the end of the campaign season, the sharpshooter battalion would be disbanded and the men would return to their parent regiments. This practice was first used in December 1862 by Brigadier General Rodes, whose skirmishers had been severely handled by the 2d USSS at Antietam/Sharpsburg. In response, Rodes ordered the 5th Alabama Volunteer Infantry's Major Eugene Blackford to raise a sharpshooter company for his brigade. When Rodes advanced to division command, he ordered each brigade to raise an ad hoc battalion; Blackford then expanded his command to battalion strength.

Judging distance drill at the Hythe School of Musketry, founded by the British Army in 1855. This illustration appeared in *The Illustrated London News* in a two-page article published in October that year. During the Civil War, most American sharpshooters' training lacked elements common to European marksmanship schools, whose curricula included such topics as weapon nomenclature, functioning of parts, disassembly and reassembly, maintenance, ballistics, sight adjustment, and – most importantly – distance estimation. The high trajectory of the Minié ball meant that even with perfect aim, a man-sized target could be missed easily if the sights were not adjusted correctly for the distance. (Universal History Archive/UIG via Getty Images)

RECRUITMENT AND TRAINING

Whether Union or Confederate, it should be remembered that not everyone who was qualified to become a sharpshooter did in fact serve as one, instead electing to remain with the company composed of men from their community. These marksmen remained with their unit unless detailed away or volunteered for ad hoc sharpshooter duty. They would, however, remain on their battalion or regiment's muster roll, much like a soldier detailed as a hospital attendant or teamster. Thus during the Civil War there were numerous instances when an officer would be called upon to provide a marksman and the officer knew which soldier could be relied upon for a long-range shot.

Union

Throughout the northern states, recruitment posters were distributed and posted announcing the creation of sharpshooter companies. The posters' promises – that the men would be excused from drilling and standing picket, and would only be used as long-range marksmen – caught the attention of many men. Along with a promise of extra pay, they were to be equipped with scoped target rifles. Another incentive was provided by the assurance that as long-range marksmen, they would fight from a distance and that they would not participate in any infantry assaults other than to provide supporting fire. These promises persuaded many of a region's best shots to come forward, using the longarm of their choice to qualify as a sharpshooter by meeting the War Department's marksmanship standard.

Once organized into companies, the newly qualified sharpshooters were assigned to a regiment or battalion and sent off to a camp of instruction where – much to their shock – they were drilled according to William J. Hardee's tactical manual *Rifle and Light Infantry Tactics: For the Exercise and Manoeuvres of Troops When Acting As Light Infantry Or Riflemen*. Like other recruits, they were taught deportment, marching, the manual of arms, and the various bugle calls, and performed camp and guard duty. Marching was especially hated. What was worse, as the volunteers did not expect to engage in close-quarter combat, they were dismayed to learn they were required to practice bayonet drill.

As the sharpshooters were to be skirmishers, there were plenty of skirmish drills where they practiced moving swiftly and how to maximize

ABOVE
With the exception of Companies C, E, and part of F, 1st USSS, the first longarm issued to Berdan's Sharpshooters was the .56-caliber Colt Root Revolving Rifle. Although its five-shot cylinder made it technically a repeater, it was much slower to reload than either the Spencer or the Henry. Its paper cartridges were susceptible to moisture. While reasonably accurate, this rifle had all the defects of a revolver including lead shaving, which could injure an adjacent soldier, and chain fire (multiple cylinders discharging with one shot), which could maim the shooter's hand. An interim longarm, it was exchanged for the Sharps. (USNPS Photo, Springfield Armory National Historic Site, SPAR 5919)

use of the terrain for cover. This suited them better and the entire regiment could deploy as skirmishers as readily as one ordinary infantry company could deploy in line of battle. The frequent target practice may have offered some compensation for the bayonet and marching drills. Unlike ordinary infantrymen, the sharpshooters enjoyed target practice and held frequent shooting competitions to hone their skills. In the 1st USSS, Company C (Michigan) and Company E (New Hampshire) brought their target rifles with them and the regiment competed for prizes with these guns. A typical day at the Camp of Instruction included nearly as much target practice (2 hours and 40 minutes) as drill (3 hours).

The recruitment inducement of extra pay was never recognized by the War Department and this was a sore point for many men. Additionally, the promise to issue .52-caliber scoped Sharps breechloading, single-shot rifles was not initially fulfilled. Originally, both the 1st and 2d USSS were issued .56-caliber Colt Root Revolving Rifles, but these were later replaced with Sharps rifles when the latter became available.

Unlike most company commanders, Captain John Saunders of the 1st Andrew Sharpshooters balked at the notion of drilling. Because his men had heavier rifles that weighed 20–32lb, Saunders considered drilling to be impractical, and so he excused his men from drill but allowed them to participate if they wanted to. When a brigade formation was called, his men often stood at parade rest in lieu of drilling with the rest of the brigade.

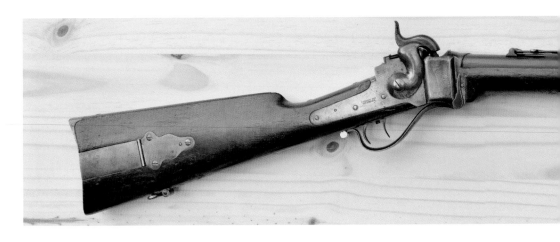

Saunders' close ties with his brigade commander, Brigadier General Frederick W. Lander, allowed Saunders to get away with it. Naturally, other brigade members resented this special arrangement and they dubbed Saunders' sharpshooters "Lander's Pets." When Saunders and his company left their Camp of Instruction, supernumeraries stayed behind and became the core of the 2d Andrew Sharpshooters, led by Captain Lewis E. Wentworth. Attached to the 22d Massachusetts Volunteer Infantry (aka "Henry Wilson's Regiment"), they were drilled according to Hardee's precepts in late July 1862.

Both companies of Andrew Sharpshooters originally carried target rifles, and emphatically rejected the Sharps rifle. After Lander's death on March 2, 1862, and the Seven Days' Battles, the men of the 1st Andrew Sharpshooters no longer enjoyed the special protection they once had. Ordered to place their target rifles into the wagons for transport, the men were then marched to Alexandria, Virginia, where they faced loaded cannon. Escape was impossible because cavalry with drawn sabers blocked the side streets. Given the choice of accepting the Sharps rifle or facing cannon fire, the men took the Sharps. It proved to be much easier for the Union authorities to convince the men of the 2d Andrew Sharpshooters to adopt the Sharps. The men's knapsacks, containing the necessary target-rifle accoutrements such as bullet molds, bullet sizers, and paper-patch cutters, had been stolen at the battle of Malvern Hill (July 1, 1862); without these items, their target rifles were useless. Given no choice, the men of the 2d Andrew Sharpshooters reluctantly accepted the Sharps rifle.

BELOW
The .52-caliber Sharps was a breechloading, single-shot rifle. Lowering the lever caused the locking block to drop and exposed the chamber for inserting a linen or skin cartridge. After inserting the cartridge, the breech was raised, slicing off the end of the cartridge and exposing the powder to ignition by either a percussion cap or a pellet primer. Quick to load, the Sharps was ideal for skirmishing as reloading the rifle did not require the soldier to expose himself as much as when reloading a rifle-musket. Adjustable sights on the Sharps could be raised to a maximum of either 700yd or 800yd and in one incident, soldiers of Berdan's Sharpshooters carved sticks so as to enable them to harass a Confederate signal tower at a range of 1,500yd. (Martin Pegler)

Confederate

The Confederates responded to Cooper's order to raise sharpshooters by numerous means. The core of any regiment was the company and most companies were based on local communities with men who were classmates, brothers, cousins, coworkers, neighbors, friends, or attended the same church serving together. Many soldiers were loath to part from one another for the company of strangers. Besides, sharpshooting was viewed as an especially dangerous role with more potential to suffer death or injury than a normal infantryman's role.

Accordingly, the Confederate authorities employed five methods to fill the ranks. The first was the transfer of entire companies; whether a company's men were qualified or not, some companies were detached and converted to sharpshooters. The second was conscription, with men of unknown quality being assigned to sharpshooter units. The third was the hiring of substitutes: until this practice was discontinued by 1863, men could pool their money and hire a substitute to go in one's place. The fourth method involved officers choosing men for sharpshooter duty. If insufficient numbers of volunteers stepped forward, men could find themselves "volunteered" by their comrades or by their officers. Finally, applicants were screened and selected for their proven loyalty, bravery, knowledge of drill, and demonstrated marksmanship.

While casualties could be high, there was always a waiting list of qualified applicants to fill sharpshooter vacancies. For sharpshooter units armed with Whitworth or Kerr rifles, each brigade maintained a list of its best shots as potential replacements. Lieutenant George H. Burton, commanding the target-rifle squad in the 1st Kentucky Brigade, selected his applicants under fire; if the man flinched, he would be returned to his company (Thompson 1898: 268).

Easily the least successful attempt to implement Cooper's order was that of Major General John C. Pemberton's Department of South Carolina, Georgia, and Florida. Upon receipt of the order, Pemberton raised the 1st and 2d South Carolina battalions Sharpshooters. According to Lieutenant Colonel John G. Pressley, the commander of the 25th South Carolina Infantry, he

> was ordered to detail twenty-four men of his command, and have them in readiness to report for duty when required. This quota was divided among the ten companies in a manner as just as possible. Each captain was directed to name the men to be detailed from his company … Every one who had a worthless fellow on his company detailed him … Unfitness for a sharpshooter was the quality most looked after. The consequence was, that as a whole, General Pemberton's sharpshooters were rivals of Falstaff's army. When gotten together it was found that after the maimed, the halt and the blind were discharged there were enough men to form two pretty good companies out of a whole battalion. (Pressley 1886: 36–38)

Pemberton's two South Carolina battalions were the exception and the Georgia battalions he raised were more creditable units. Virtually all of the state-recognized battalions were raised by the transferring of existing companies. In the Army of Northern Virginia, most battalions were raised on an ad hoc basis, with the men being detailed during the campaign season and returning to their parent units for winter quarters. Generally, each battalion was three to four companies strong.

Once selected, the Confederate sharpshooter was sent to a separate camp. The men were divided into groups of four. Their bonds were strengthened through drill which included marching, the manual of arms, and especially skirmish drills. Company- and later battalion-level drills were also undertaken.

Depending on when and where a soldier became a sharpshooter, he might receive marksmanship instruction. Two manuals were used by the Confederate armies. One, *A System for Conducting Musketry Instruction*, was based on a British manual from the Hythe School of Musketry, and was later copied by Major Calhoun Benham and printed in Richmond in 1863. The other was a pamphlet (now lost) based on the French *École de Tir* (shooting school) at Vincennes, prepared by Cadmus M. Wilcox and likely an adaptation of his antebellum book on the same subject, *Rifles and Rifle Practices*, published in 1859. Both manuals included distance-estimation drill, as described by Captain William S. Dunlop of McGowan's Sharpshooters, an ad hoc battalion:

> The battalion was first put on a drill in estimating distance. It was drawn up in line in open field; a man or an object the size of a man was stationed in front at an unknown distance, about 100 yards off, and the roll called; at the call of each name the man stepped forward ten paces, surveyed carefully the object in the front, calculated the intervening space, and deliberately announced in exact figures his estimate of the distance between, and a record was made of his judgment; then the next in the same way, and so on through the entire command. The distance was increased from time to time, from one hundred to two, three, five and nine hundred yards, and an accurate account kept of each man's judgment in each drill. The practice in this drill was continued from day to day until every man could tell, almost to a mathematical certainty, the distance at any given point within the compass of his drill. A few, however, were naturally and hopelessly deficient in their powers of estimating distance, and hence, were exchanged for others. (Dunlop 1899: 19–20)

Corporal Edom T. Moon, serving with the 35th Georgia Infantry, explained that each man whispered his estimate of the range to the officer conducting the exercise, taking care that the other men did not hear his answer; each soldier's estimate was recorded against his name (Koonce 2000: 137). After the men had mastered range estimation, they practiced long-range shooting, as described by Dunlop:

> The battalion was formed on the range, a target about the size of a man was placed to front at a distance of one hundred yards, with a bullseye in the center of about five inches in diameter enclosed within an inner circle of about fourteen inches and an outer circle of about twenty-four inches, a tripod was constructed of convenient height, with a sandbag lodged in its fork on which to rest the heavy rifle, while the soldier aimed and fired, and the practice began. (Dunlop 1899: 20–23)

While the course of fire prescribed by the English musketry manual required 60 rounds to be fired throughout the course, some Confederate sharpshooters shot much fewer than that. In a letter home, Sergeant Marion H. Fitzpatrick, 45th Georgia Infantry, recounted that he fired two shots at 600yd one day and then another two shots the next day (McCrea 1992: 482).

Henry Heth, shown here as colonel of the 45th Virginia Infantry, was the first officer in the United States to implement the teaching methodology of the Hythe School of Musketry. Pledging his allegiance to the Confederacy, Heth would achieve the rank of major general, fighting in numerous battles until the South's surrender in April 1865. Heth's friend Winfield S. Hancock, later to serve as a Union general, sent his fellow officer the two-page article published in *The Illustrated London News* in October 1855. Heth drew upon the article to train his company and to gain experience. He also relied on a French marksmanship manual to draft his instructions and submitted them to the War Department in February, 1858. Secretary of War John B. Floyd authorized its adoption almost immediately (March 1, 1858) and it was published by Henry Carey Baird in Pennsylvania. When the war broke out, the manual was republished by the Government Printing Office on the order of Secretary of War Edwin M. Stanton almost in its entirety, but with all references to Heth deleted. With the possible exception of the 1st Michigan Sharpshooters, there is no evidence that this manual was used by the Union for training sharpshooters. (Library of Congress)

The British musketry manual advocated the use of flags, with the shots denoted by different-colored flags that were raised above the trench. The flags eliminated the need to walk downrange to inspect the target and expedited the training. Additional training included movements to repel cavalry with bayonets and other movements for maneuver. The men were controlled through bugle calls from Hardee's *Rifle and Light Infantry Tactics* manual or with hand signals, the latter allowing for silent commands to coordinate covert movement.

There is one small group of Confederate sharpshooters who should not be overlooked – slaves. Some of the African-American slaves who accompanied their masters to war as manservants, cooks, musicians, or teamsters shouldered a gun and fought. Until March 1865, however, Confederate law forbade the enlistment of African-American soldiers. Notwithstanding the law, slaves taking up arms and fighting was a matter between the master and the slave. There are numerous accounts of African-American Confederates fighting as sharpshooters at the siege of Yorktown in 1862 and at Suffolk, Virginia, and Battery Wagner on Morris Island, South Carolina, in 1863. Southern laws prohibiting African Americans from owning firearms applied to freemen and not to slaves who could, at their master's discretion, be entrusted with firearms. This is how slaves such as Holt Collier became expert shots and when allowed to fight, were deadly accurate.

An evolution of the Volcanic repeating arms, the Henry lever-action, breechloading rifle fired a .44-caliber, 216-grain bullet in a rimfire copper cartridge propelled by 25 grains of FF black powder. The 15-shot magazine tube was open on the bottom, which made it susceptible to dirt; extra care was required of the user to ensure the dirt did not inhibit the magazine's function. While all Henrys made were eagerly bought up, it was issued in limited numbers by the Ordnance Department and most Henrys were purchased by the private soldier at $42 apiece. Birge's Western Sharpshooters purchased Henrys, which replaced the sporting guns originally provided to them. Some Henrys were captured and used by Confederates, but the Confederacy did not have the technology to produce cartridges. (USNPS Photo, Springfield Armory National Historic Site, SPAR 8119)

SHARPSHOOTER ROLES AND TACTICS

Unfortunately, the availability of sharpshooters to battlefield commanders did not necessarily mean they were deployed in that role. For example, although the sole Confederate sharpshooter regiment, the Palmetto Sharpshooters, had been intended to serve in roles akin to those played by Berdan's regiments, in the event the shortage of Confederate manpower meant that the regiment always fought in the line of battle instead of serving as dedicated skirmishers. In the Midwest, it was not uncommon for the Confederate Army of Tennessee to deploy its sharpshooter battalions as regular infantry. Furthermore, there was no doctrine that distinguished between sharpshooters who were expert skirmishers and sharpshooters acting as snipers. Most officers on both sides felt that the former role was more suitable and the latter was akin to murder.

At first, the Union sharpshooters' effectiveness was hampered by the ignorance of many officers about their deployment. For instance, during the opening stages of Major General George B. McClellan's Peninsula Campaign

(March–July 1862), the Union march up the Yorktown Peninsula from Bethel, Virginia, saw both target rifle-armed companies (C and E) of the 1st USSS serving as flankers. The companies armed with the Colt Root Revolving Rifle would have been more suitable for this task as their weapons could offer a rapidity of fire unsurpassed by most single-shot firearms. Additionally, a target rifle could weigh up to 32lb, making it fatiguing to carry during mobile warfare; moreover, such weapons normally were slow to reload.

Skirmishing

Most Civil War sharpshooters were armed with standard-issue firearms no better than those of their infantry brethren and fought in a manner akin to Napoleonic-era light infantry or riflemen. These sharpshooters often found themselves in the forefront of battle. They probed the enemy and screened the main body from attack or surprise. Frequently, they would meet head on with the enemy's skirmishers and vie with them for battlefield domination – or at least to deny it to their foe. Intended to employ sharpshooters to screen a larger unit, Hardee's skirmishing tactics enabled the skirmish officer to deploy skirmishers to the front, flank, extended or close interval, to relieve or maneuver them, firing, rallying into various formations, and battalion-scale skirmishing. In the attack skirmishers screened the main body from the enemy and denied the latter the advantage of the terrain. In the defense, skirmishers impeded the enemy's advance, allowing for the main body to receive the enemy or retreat. Unlike line infantry, skirmishers deployed in open order, allowing them to use any natural cover offered by the terrain. The smallest subgroup consisted of four skirmishers and the largest could be an entire battalion.

When they were not fighting, sharpshooters could be scouting and reporting their observations. Alternatively, they served as the rearguard, protecting against intrusions that threatened the main body. Confederate sharpshooters became experts at raiding and in their most spectacular raid (October 30, 1864) netted almost 250 prisoners. These skirmisher-type

A Union skirmish line. Skirmishing was something taught and practiced by all infantrymen on both sides of the Civil War. Skirmishers preceded the battle line, either to drive in the enemy's skirmishers or to delay or to deny the ground to them. The open-order nature of skirmishing allowed the skirmisher to take advantage of the terrain for cover or concealment. Simultaneously, it reduced target density as opposed to the line of battle where soldiers stood elbow to elbow and fought in that manner. (Martin Pegler)

sharpshooters also fought against artillery and at times dominated them. Since most cannons were muzzle-loading, their use in battle required the gunners to expose themselves to enemy small-arms fire, and it was not unknown for sharpshooters to silence artillery by driving the gunners away. Reportedly, one Berdan sharpshooter fired at the sandbags protecting the Confederate gunners and in so doing threw enough sand into the bore to create an obstruction that burst the gun when it was fired. In other incidents, sharpshooters annoyed the personnel of an artillery battery so much that the gunners engaged in a duel to rid themselves of the sharpshooting pests. During sieges the threat posed by sharpshooters to the gunners became so dangerous that artillery pieces had to be protected by fortifications, rope curtains, iron plates, or even sandbags thrown into the embrasure so that the guns could be reloaded.

Sharpshooters also set their sights on signalmen, and drove them from their towers, hampering the enemy's communication. Gunboats close to shore closed their gun ports for fear of incoming rifle bullets. Some gunboats were even captured thanks to the help of sharpshooters. Siege warfare placed a premium on marksmanship and the sharpshooter became indispensable. Many techniques pioneered during the Civil War were later rediscovered in the trenches of World War I. Along with camouflage, methods of outwitting one's opponent at the opposing loophole, metal-reinforced loopholes, angled loopholes instead of loopholes that looked straight on, and even the primitive equivalent of the periscope rifle were all pioneered during the Civil War.

Sniping

The sharpshooter equipped with a target or scoped rifle did not quite fit with the 19th-century military mind. Only a handful of officers understood how to use such troops, and no tactical doctrine was written to explain how best to harness their potential. Among the Union generals who understood how to use sharpshooters with specialized rifles were Brigadier General Frederick W. Lander, Major General Frank Wheaton, and Brigadier General Régis de Trobriand, while among their Confederate counterparts Brigadier General Johnson Hagood, Major General Patrick R. Cleburne, and others saw their potential. The vast majority of Civil War-era officers were ignorant of how best to use sharpshooters, however, and it would take another 50 years for the trench warfare of World War I to cement the sniper doctrine. Even among the officers who were aware of its potential, such as the Union's Lander and Berdan and the Confederacy's Cleburne, their influence outside of their immediate command was limited. Other officers were morally repugnant at the notion of shooting an enemy soldier who presented no direct harm to them. The sharpshooters' mode of warfare was believed to be no better than murder and the bias against this mode of warfare endured for over a century.

A famous painting by Winslow Homer (1836–1910), *Sharpshooter on Duty in the Army of the Potomac*, is illustrative of their genre and their mode of fighting. Major General John Sedgwick, the commander of the Union's VI Corps at the battle of Spotsylvania Court House (May 9, 1864), is the most famous commanding officer struck down by an unseen foe. Ironically, Sedgwick disliked this mode of warfare and had he promoted it, could have prevented his death. While probably not armed with anything other than a

Pattern 1853 Enfield rifle-musket, one Confederate sharpshooter at Lieutenant General Jubal A. Early's assault on Washington, DC (July 12, 1864) almost hit Lincoln while the Union President stood atop the parapet at Fort Stevens. Luckily for the Union and Lincoln, the Confederate sharpshooter hit and wounded Surgeon C.V.V. Crawford who stood next to the President.

It was not until sometime around 1864 that target rifle-armed sharpshooters began to receive differential treatment from commanding officers. They were given more freedom of action to choose their own ground, were excused from picket duty, or – unlike one unfortunate target rifle-armed Union company at Mine Run (November 27–December 2, 1863) – were excused from infantry charges. The distinction between the two types of sharpshooters was universally understood by both sides by 1864, but for many soldiers of the 1st and 2d USSS it was too late. Attrition had already reduced their numbers.

Even when telescopic sight-equipped sharpshooters demonstrated their effectiveness, they could be rearmed with standard-issue weapons, meaning that the lessons learned and expertise gained were quickly forgotten as they once again resumed their positions among the ranks. The Confederate sharpshooters who fought at Morris Island in 1863 suffered this fate, but the men under Cleburne's command were spared because of his special interest in sharpshooting.

Ranging in weight from 14lb up to 32lb, a wide variety of target rifles were fielded during the Civil War. This example, manufactured as a flintlock by Barnes of Boston, was converted to caplock and a full-length brass scope was added *c*.1850. It was carried by a Kentucky sharpshooter during the Civil War. There is no one rifle that typifies these heavy-barrel firearms. Some were equipped with iron sights and other had optical sights. Each had to be accompanied by a custom bullet mold, a swedge to size the bullet, patch cutter, false muzzle-loading device, and sometimes a rest. The rifles were cased for transport. (Martin Pegler)

Use of camouflage

Camouflage predates the Civil War sharpshooter. Precedents may be found in camouflage used by European skirmishers, notably the dark-green uniforms worn by British riflemen in the Napoleonic Wars. European sportsmen were also aware of the advantage of camouflage and stalked in tree-like blinds or animal suits in pursuit of game. In Colonial America, the Native Americans taught the colonists the value of camouflage and some frontiersmen wore frocks that were dyed in walnut husks so as to blend with the woods; thus the proposal that Berdan's Sharpshooters be clad in green during the summer months and grayish-brown in the winter was nothing novel, but in accordance with tradition. Originally, Berdan's Sharpshooters were clothed in green kepis and coats (their black rubber buttons did not shine like the polished brass buttons of their infantry brethren). Initially, they were issued blue trousers, but these were replaced when green ones became available; brown gaiters were also issued. By 1864, uniform standards had suffered, according to Major Charles P. Mattocks, the commanding officer of the 1st USSS (quoted in Racine 1994: 112–13).

The Springfield rifle-musket was the most-issued infantry arm of the Civil War. Weighing 9¼lb, this single-shot muzzle-loader had a 39in barrel; its .578-caliber, 535-grain Minié bullet was propelled by 60 grains of powder and was capable of penetrating 4in of pine at 1,000yd; its bore varied from .580 to .5825. Early versions – this is the Model 1855 – had a ladder sight, brass storage box, and the Maynard Tape Primer ignition system; later versions discarded the ladder sight for a simpler folding leaf sight. (USNPS Photo, Springfield Armory National Historic Site, SPAR 931)

The men of the 1st New York Sharpshooters wore blue uniforms, but with the same black rubber buttons worn by Berdan's regiments; an example is displayed at the Atlanta Historical Center. Other sharpshooter units are not known to have been issued distinctive uniforms and paintings by the aforementioned Winslow Homer, Julian A. Scott (1846–1901), and even Alfred Bellard (1843–91) depict blue-clad sharpshooters. The 1st Michigan Sharpshooters were attired in the standard blue infantry uniform, but dirtied their uniforms by rolling themselves on the ground before battle – a camouflage technique they learned from the Native Americans serving in the unit. The early-war uniforms worn by Birge's Western Sharpshooters are described as "gray uniforms of felt, with close-fitting skull caps, and buffalo-skin knapsacks and a powder-horn" (Coffin 1887: 92); another observer, Frank B. Willke of *The New York Times*, added that their caps had black-dyed squirrel tails (Logsdon 1999: 9). Later images of Birge's Western Sharpshooters do not show any unique clothing.

Confederate sharpshooters received no special clothing allowance, with soldiers procuring their "uniforms" from their quartermaster, home, clothing found around camp, and the battlefield. The Confederate uniform with its various shades of gray or hues of "butternut" also blended well with the terrain. Although tests conducted by the King's Royal Rifle Corps (a British rifle unit) suggested that gray objects were less visible on the battlefield, the Confederate use of gray was probably incidental and related to the color used for many militia uniforms before 1861. Butternut was accepted because of the lack of other available dyes and not because of any desire for camouflage. Fortunately, it blended well; Private John W. Haley, 17th Maine Volunteer Infantry, described one group of Confederates as being clad in ragged garments that blended with the hues of the Virginian landscape (Silliker 1985: 260). The only distinguishing feature on the Confederate sharpshooter's uniform would be the special badge indicating his status as a sharpshooter, but no evidence has been found supporting the proposition that Confederate sharpshooters outside of the Army of Northern Virginia wore special identifying badges on their uniform. Blackford's sharpshooters wore a red trefoil, and Brigadier General William McRae's sharpshooters a gold cross; Brigadier General Samuel McGowan's sharpshooters had a diagonal red band with a red star above it, and Brigadier General George H. Steuart's brigade had a red quatrefoil over a black octagon-shaped patch.

When needed, some sharpshooters took pains to conceal themselves, one Confederate soldier, John West, recalling that he pinned leaves on his clothing to aid concealment when stationed in a tree (Morrow 1989: 42–43). Wyman S. White of Berdan's Sharpshooters learned camouflage from a Native American serving in a Michigan regiment he met (White 1993: 249–50). White expressed his wish to move through a cornfield into the cover of some brush, but could not see how he could move through the field without being spotted. Cutting off some stalks of corn, the Native American showed White how to insert them into his clothes and equipment. After camouflaging themselves in this fashion, the two men were able to make their way across the field and into the cover of the bushes; they then successfully targeted a Confederate artillery battery, denying the enemy gunners access to their pieces all afternoon. It is likely that White's Native American companion was a soldier with the 1st Michigan Sharpshooters. Serving in that unit's Company K, Sergeant Thomas Ke-chi-ti-go, also known as "Big Tom," also instructed his men to cover their breasts and head with twigs and leaves.

In another incident, Corporal Edom T. Moon's comrades in the 35th Georgia Infantry used camouflage to ambush African-American soldiers fighting for the

A group of soldiers armed with .577-caliber Pattern 1853 Enfield rifle-muskets. The soldiers' use of civilian clothing may have been colorful, but it was often fatally conspicuous. The image has been reverse-printed. After the Springfield and its variants, the Enfield was the second most common infantry arm used in the Civil War. Besides being made in Britain, copycats were made in Belgium and sold to both sides. The quality could be variable, though, and many sold to both the Union and the Confederacy were shoddily made. Hammers could be too brittle and break under usage. The same could be said of some nipples that shattered when used. Overall, though, the "Enfields" gave good service. (Library of Congress)

Born on January 28, 1831 in Oldtown, Maine, stonemason Ira Lunt enlisted into Company D, 2d USSS, on September 2, 1864. On November 24, 1864, at considerable expense ($125), he bought a rifle built by Malcom W. Long, and requested permission to use it in lieu of the standard Sharps rifle. His request was approved by Brigadier General Régis de Trobriand and Major General Gershom Mott. When the 2d USSS was disbanded on February 20, 1865, Lunt was transferred to Company A, 17th Maine Volunteer Infantry, and fought at Petersburg (February 20– April 2) and Sayler's Creek (April 6) before witnessing Lee's surrender at Appomattox (April 9). Honorably discharged on June 10, 1865, in 1875 Lunt moved to New Castle, Delaware, where he continued his trade as a stonemason; his granite icebreakers still stand in the Delaware River today. Lunt was active in the postwar veterans' organization, The Grand Army of the Republic. He died on July 15, 1915 in Wilmington, Delaware. (Thomas Lunt)

Markings on the barrel of Lunt's rifle tell us that it was made by O. Huse of Manchester, New Hampshire and the gun assembled by M.W. Long of Bangor, Maine. (Thomas Lunt)

Union (Wood n.d.: 61). Moon and six others dug a rifle pit under cover of darkness, camouflaging it with pine brush. In the morning, Moon coaxed the enemy soldiers into the open on the pretense of exchanging newspapers. When they left their trenches and approached with intent to barter, Moon gave the signal and the concealed Confederates shot the hapless men down. The same tactic was practiced on a larger scale by Cleburne's division at Ringgold Gap (November 27, 1863). Fighting as a rearguard for General Braxton Bragg's retreating Army of Tennessee, Cleburne hid his shot-loaded cannon with brush. His men were ordered to lie down and to conceal themselves. When the unwary Union soldiers approached to within 100yd, the cannon were unmasked and fired a volley at close range. Cleburne's men rose and delivered a volley, driving back the stunned Union soldiers; his victory earned him the sobriquet "Stonewall of the West."

In June 1864, one Confederate sharpshooter used natural light for concealment to harass artillery crews of Battery G, 1st New York Light Artillery at Fort Morton, Petersburg (Ames 2000: 125–26). Taking care to fire only when the setting sun was at his back and in the faces of his enemy, the sharpshooter shot between two and six Union soldiers each day, killing First Lieutenant Albert N. Ames and Private John McCann; the Confederate took position in a pine tree, meaning that only the smoke from each of his shots was visible to the Union artillerists. Unfortunately for the men of the Union battery, they were not permitted to fire back.

Stalking

Sharpshooters also resorted to stalking their prey:

> The sharpshooter would take up his position, and, cat like, patiently watch for his victim, whose appearance, although but momentary, was the signal of his death. The endurance of the sharpshooter is remarkable. Seated on a bough of a tree, in a ruined chimney, or in any other position where they could see without being seen, they have been known to remain in the same position for hours, without food, with their eye fixed on one particular object – the spot where the expected victim was to make his appearance. (Anon 1864: 85)

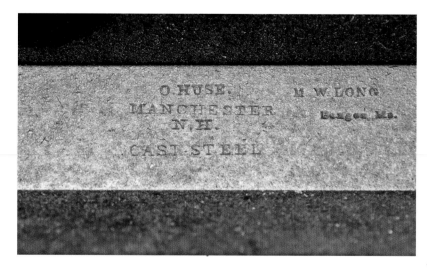

Maneuvering into a position without detection was described by one Confederate soldier, John Hatton, who stated that he saw a friendly sharpshooter moving cautiously up a slope, crawling and pushing his rifle ahead of him (West 1995: 102). Upon reaching a suitable spot, the sharpshooter rose to his knees to get a view of the enemy; he repeated this until he found the optimal position, then fired his rifle, immediately pushing his weapon down the slope and sliding after it to safety.

At the siege of Yorktown, Brigadier General Régis de Trobriand came across one soldier:

> A few steps from there I saw a young soldier lying motionless, flat on the ground, a man of a mild and inoffensive nature. His disposition was in accordance with his physical appearance, and he would have been averse to killing even a sheep. But the man chase had transformed him. With his head covered with leaves, and at the level of the earth, he had crept out there with his eyes intently fixed upon a single point of the swamp, watching as a wild beast of prey watches for his concealed victim. His loaded gun was pushed out in front of him, looking like a stick lying on the stones, but really directed under his hand, upon the bunch of brushes which absorbed his attention. (de Trobriand 1899: 180)

Another view of Lunt's rifle. The large knob upon which the rear of the scope body rests is for sight elevation. Note the two-trigger arrangement. The rear trigger is pressed first, making the front or set trigger very light. Today, this rifle is in the possession of Ira Lunt's great-great-grandson, Tom Lunt. (Thomas Lunt)

The 1861 wartime production of the Springfield rifle-musket saw further simplification with the elimination of the Maynard Tape Primer system. Both the 1st Michigan Sharpshooters and Captain Richard Ela's sharpshooters at the siege of Battery Wagner (July 19–September 6, 1863) carried Springfields. (USNPS Photo, Springfield Armory National Historic Site, SPAR 928)

Perhaps the best stalkers in the Union Army were its Native American soldiers. When one Confederate sharpshooter annoyed Brigadier General Orlando B. Willcox's headquarters staff in June 1864, they sent for a sharpshooter. A Native American known to history as One Eye responded and, asking nothing of anyone, sat down and watched. After a half-hour, he rose, walked off, and sometime later the pickets reported a Confederate falling from a tree; One Eye reported his success (Herek 1998: 171). In another incident a Confederate sharpshooter pinned down a Union soldier. The Confederate patiently waited for the enemy soldier to expose himself, but suddenly found himself staring into the muzzle of the Yankee's gun. He had heard of the Native Americans' stalking ability, but thought himself immune (Abernethy 1958: 79–80). At Vicksburg, Major Joseph Stockton, 72d Illinois Volunteer Infantry, recalled the activities of Native American sharpshooters of the 14th Wisconsin Volunteer Infantry (Wheeler 1978: 202). These marksmen disguised their heads with leaves and crawled cautiously across the battlefield, each man usually taking position behind a suitable log. Their fire successfully suppressed the Confederate artillery. Similarly, Captain John G.B. Adams, 19th Massachusetts Volunteer Infantry, who fought at Spotsylvania

Court House's Bloody Angle on May 12, 1864, vividly remembered a Native American soldier stalking out in the open: "When we were relieved by the 6th Corps the 6th Wisconsin was in our front. One of their men was an Indian. He would crawl near the rebel line, wait until they fired, then fire and drag himself back. He could hardly be seen above the ground" (Adams 1899: 93).

Arguably the best example of stalking by Native American sharpshooters was witnessed by Private George Hitchcock of the 21st Massachusetts Volunteer Infantry (Hitchcock 1997: 304–05). Hitchcock related how one particularly exposed Union post was surrounded by enemy positions on three sides, with one especially troublesome Confederate sharpshooter taking a toll on the soldiers manning it. As he surveyed the shrub-covered ground ahead of the Union position, Hitchcock was startled to see one of the shrubs had changed position, but with no evidence of movement. After a half-hour of such activity, there was a flash from the shrub and the Confederate sharpshooter was hit; having successfully stalked and hit his target, the Native American marksman jumped up and raced back to the Union line.

A .577-caliber Pattern 1856 Enfield two-band rifle with 33in barrel. Whereas other longarms including the Springfield were accurate out to 500yd, the Enfield could reach 900yd. Both the longer 39in three-band and the 33in two-band sergeants' rifle were used by Confederate sharpshooters, but the latter was especially reserved for them. (USNPS Photo, Springfield Armory National Historic Site, SPAR 4552)

A Pritchett-pattern Minié bullet. Unlike the US Army, which adopted the Minié ball with its grease grooves, the British Army adopted a smooth-sided bullet called the Pritchett, also used by the Confederacy. (Martin Pegler)

LEADERSHIP AND COMMUNICATIONS

In the Union armies, captaincies were given to those men who applied to the state governor for permission to raise a company. The captain appointed recruiting officers (lieutenants) who went to various towns seeking recruits. Once the company was raised, the state governor would confirm their ranks and they were sworn into federal service. In the volunteer service, the men elected their field officers. Their elections would then be confirmed by the governor of the state of their origin. Sometimes the field officer would be offered a tentative position and upon raising of the regiment and confirmation by election, he would then receive his commission. While Union officers were later examined on their knowledge of Hardee's *Rifle and Light Infantry Tactics*, familiarity with this work did not necessarily ensure that an officer was a good leader; Hiram Berdan, who always found lawful means to excuse himself from the battlefield or from fighting, was despised by his men for his cowardice. Other men, such as Captain (later Colonel) Casper Trepp or Chaplain Lorenzo Barber, the fighting parson of the 2d USSS, were highly respected. The men of the 1st USSS envied the 2d USSS because Barber not only tended to the men's spiritual needs, but also shouldered a rifle and fought alongside them.

Confederate sharpshooter officers came from two sources. If the company in question was raised at war's outbreak, the men elected their officers and if said company was converted to sharpshooters, their officers were now sharpshooter officers. If a unit was later raised afresh or in the field (ad hoc), the officers were generally selected by the person who raised the unit. If said officer was not already commissioned, his commission was subject to approval by the Confederate Congress. Men such as Major Eugene Blackford, Major Thomas L. Wooten, Captain William S. Dunlop, Lieutenant Abraham B. Schell, and Lieutenant George H. Burton were selected for their bravery, knowledge of drill, and leadership qualities.

As a rule, successful sharpshooter officers had to be skilled skirmishers who could direct their skirmish line effectively while under fire. Bravery was essential and Sergeant Berry Benson of McGowan's Sharpshooters recalled one skulking lieutenant, who was removed once reported (Benson 1992: 181). He was the exception to the rule that sharpshooter officers were distinguished by their enthusiasm, bravery, and intelligence (Young 1996: 270).

The human voice only carries clearly so far; as Major Eugene Blackford, 5th Alabama Infantry, complained, it was difficult for officers and NCOs to relay orders verbally, given the distances involved (Ray 2006: 47). Vocal commands had to compete against the roar of musketry and cannons and could be unintelligible, especially for soldiers at the far end of the skirmish line. On the other hand, the bugle could be readily distinguished and Hardee directed that "The movement will be habitually indicated by the sounds of the bugle" (Hardee 1861: §10). Similarly, the Union sharpshooters were also directed by bugle calls. In the absence of field officers, Major Charles Mattocks, 17th Maine Volunteer Infantry, briefly commanded the 1st USSS; in a letter home, Mattocks praised his men's familiarity with the bugle calls used during skirmish drill (Racine 1994: 126). In the Midwest, Birge's Western Sharpshooters were trained to respond to hand signals, to aid covert movement on the battlefield.

Fredericksburg

December 11–15, 1862

BACKGROUND TO BATTLE

Disappointed by Major General George B. McClellan's failure to pursue and destroy General Robert E. Lee's Army of Northern Virginia after the battle of Antietam/Sharpsburg (September 17, 1862), President Lincoln relieved McClellan as commander of the Army of the Potomac on November 7, 1862, and replaced him with a reluctant Major General Ambrose E. Burnside. Burnside proposed to steal a march on Lee. Instead of marching along the Orange Plank Road, the toll road between the mountains of Virginia and Fredericksburg, as McClellan would have done, Burnside would quietly withdraw his army and march south to Falmouth, Virginia, across the Rappahannock River from Fredericksburg. Waiting pontoons would then be thrown across to bridge the Rappahannock and Fredericksburg immediately occupied. Burnside's wagons would be loaded with 12 days' provisions and he would march south and capture Richmond, Virginia before Lee could catch him.

Pictured here with his staff, Major General Edwin V. Sumner (center) commanded the Army of the Potomac's Right Grand Division, composed of Major General Darius N. Couch's II Corps and Brigadier General Orlando B. Willcox's IX Corps. (© CORBIS/Corbis via Getty Images)

Lincoln approved of Burnside's plan and thought it could succeed if implemented rapidly. With Lincoln's approval, Burnside sent for the pontoon train and set his army, 127,574 strong, in motion (Palfrey 2002: 138). Elements of the Union army first reached Falmouth on November 17, but the pontoon train had not yet arrived. While Fredericksburg was only lightly held by the Confederates,

Roughly halfway between Washington, DC and Richmond, the town of Fredericksburg was founded in the 17th century. Its access to the Rappahannock River made it an important commercial center with mills and warehouses for export of tobacco and other goods as well as imports from Britain. A dam upriver near Falmouth on the opposite bank controlled the flow of water, making Fredericksburg an ideal site for an industrial town. The town and its c.5,000 inhabitants successfully avoided the Civil War until the arrival of the Army of the Potomac. Spanning the river was a bridge built before 1861 by the Richmond, Fredericksburg and Potomac Railroad. While the bridge had been destroyed early in the conflict, its pylons still stood over the river as mute testimony to a more peaceful time. This photograph shows Fredericksburg after the railroad bridge was destroyed, as viewed from the eastern shore of the Rappahannock River. (Photo 12/UIG via Getty Images)

Burnside was unsure of the garrison's size and reluctant to commit small forces to take the town. His hesitancy allowed Lee to move Lieutenant General James Longstreet's 38,320-strong corps from Falmouth down to Fredericksburg on November 23 and entrench it along Marye's Heights, a ridge that dominated Fredericksburg. Over the next three days, the Union pontoons finally begin to trickle in.

At this point of the war, Lee was still licking his wounds after Antietam and had no further offensive plans. Instead, he would recover his strength and react to any Union thrust. With McClellan, Lee at least had a predictable opponent, but Burnside was unknown and this caused Lee some concern. When Lee realized that he faced the entire Army of the Potomac, he ordered Lieutenant General Thomas J. "Stonewall" Jackson at Winchester to join him with his 37,000-strong corps. Upon Jackson's arrival on December 1, he was sent downriver from Fredericksburg to guard against any Union attempt to cross the Rappahannock there. By this point the pontoons had arrived and Burnside had lost the element of surprise. Nevertheless, Burnside ordered his engineers to commence building the bridges in the early-morning hours of December 11.

Defending Fredericksburg was Brigadier General William Barksdale's Mississippi Brigade. Barksdale confidently told Lee that if he wanted to cross the Rappahannock River, it could be over the bodies of dead Yankees. Knowing that the town was the crossing point, Barksdale reinforced the 17th Mississippi Infantry with ten picked marksmen from the 13th Mississippi Infantry. As they have never been identified, nothing is known about the ten sharpshooters from the 13th Mississippi Infantry. It is known that prior to Fredericksburg, the 13th Mississippi fought at First Bull Run/Manassas, the Seven Days' Battles, Second Bull Run/Manassas, and Antietam/Sharpsburg, much of it while being part of Barksdale's Brigade. No stranger to combat, their regimental commander would know who among his men were the best marksmen. Barksdale's men concealed themselves in trenches, behind

makeshift barricades, and in the homes that lined the waterfront and waited patiently as the construction noise carried across the river.

Fighting against them were the 1st Andrew Sharpshooters. Originally equipped with target telescope rifles, the 1st Andrew Sharpshooters were bloodied at Ball's Bluff (October 21, 1861) where they crossed the Potomac and Edward's Ferry and were credited for driving back an entire Confederate regiment (the Confederates conducted only a feint). They fought at Yorktown and some of the Seven Days' Battles. Dissatisfied with the service, they signed a petition asking to be discharged and presented it to their army commander, Major General McClellan. McClellan spoke with their representative, Lieutenant Emerson L. Bicknell, who explained how the sharpshooters, unlike regular infantry, could not march with their rifles. McClellan said that wagons would be provided for carrying their guns and dismissed Bicknell.

While the Union army moved from the Yorktown Peninsula to Alexandria, it was decided that the sharpshooters would be more useful as skirmishers and they were ordered at cannon point to adopt the Sharps rifle. While the sharpshooters were loath to fight as skirmishers and wanted their discharge, the cannons aimed at them along with cavalry cutting off their retreat gave them little choice. To prevent assassinations, they were not issued ammunition until a few days later.

The 1st Andrew Sharpshooters arrived at, but did not fight at, Second Bull Run/Manassas. As part of Brigadier General Alfred Sully's First Brigade in Brigadier General Oliver O. Howard's 2d Division of Major General Darius N. Couch's II Corps, their next battle was Antietam/Sharpsburg. At the extreme end of the Union line at the West Woods, they were outflanked and suffered huge casualties. Among their losses were Captain John Saunders – likely murdered by one of his own men whom he had disciplined – Lieutenant Berry, and eight other men; nine more would die from their wounds. At Fredericksburg, they received a new captain, William Plummer, along with 40 new recruits, some of whom brought target rifles with them.

MAP KEY

1 0200hrs, December 11: With Confederate pickets having reported noises of heavy objects being moved at 2200hrs the previous evening, Brigadier General William Barksdale reports to Major General Lafayette McLaws, his divisional commander, that Union pontoons are being placed in the water. McLaws instructs Barksdale to permit the work to continue unhindered so as to commit the Union engineers to laying the bridges. Major Wesley Brainerd of the 50th New York Engineers estimates that it will take three hours to build two bridges.

2 0430hrs, December 11: By this time the bridges are halfway across the Rappahannock River. Captain John P.W. Read's artillery battery on Marye's Heights fires to signal that Barksdale's men should commence firing. They do so and sweep the Union bridge-builders off their unfinished bridges.

3 1000hrs, December 11: Frustrated that his bridge-builders have been stymied, Major General Ambrose E. Burnside unleashes an artillery barrage on the town. Personnel of the Andrew Sharpshooters, the 7th Michigan Volunteer Infantry, and the 19th Massachusetts Volunteer Infantry rush to the waterfront and begin firing at the smoke signatures of Barksdale's Confederates. Several times the bridge-builders attempt to finish their work, but are driven back each time by the Confederate sharpshooters.

4 1430hrs, December 11: The 7th Michigan, the first of four Union regiments ordered to perform an amphibious assault after the failure of the Union barrage to drive off the Confederate sharpshooters, establishes a bridgehead on the western shore of the Rappahannock and begins suppressing the Confederate sharpshooters. At 1450hrs, the 19th Michigan also lands and expands the bridgehead held by the 7th Michigan.

5 1515hrs, December 11: The 89th New York Volunteer Infantry lands at the lower crossing between Princess Elizabeth Street and Frederick Street, opposed by the 18th and 21st Mississippi Infantry.

6 1520hrs, December 11: The 20th Massachusetts Volunteer Infantry lands at the bridgehead held by the 7th Michigan and 19th Massachusetts. Other units including the 59th New York, 106th Pennsylvania, and 127th Pennsylvania Volunteer Infantry arrive as reinforcements.

7 1600hrs, December 11: The 20th Massachusetts advances up Hawke Street toward Caroline Street and is joined by the 7th Michigan and 19th Massachusetts in house-to-house fighting. Almost simultaneously, the 106th Pennsylvania leads the charge south to clear the Confederates along Water Street. South of these units, the 89th New York advances along Frederick and Princess Elizabeth streets, capturing the 8th Florida Infantry, which failed to get the order to retreat and is cut off.

8 1845hrs, December 11: Barksdale begins to withdraw his brigade, leaving the 21st Mississippi as a rearguard. With the waterfront secured, the bridge-builders begin finishing the bridges. At 1900hrs, Brigadier General Oliver O. Howard's 2d Division (II Corps, Right Grand Division) is the first Union division to cross. On December 12, Burnside moves the rest of his army across the Rappahannock and deploys for battle.

9 Dawn, December 13: The last of Jackson's men arrive. Union forces attack Jackson's line and break through, but are unsupported and must concede their gains. The Union's Right Grand Division (II Corps and IX Corps) attacks Longstreet's Confederates at Marye's Heights and is driven back repeatedly. The armies remain in position on December 14; on December 15, the Union forces withdraw across the Rappahannock.

Battlefield environment

Dominating Fredericksburg from 600yd distance was Marye's Heights, named after the Marye family that owned the land there. From Marye's Heights, artillery could sweep the open area between the feature and the town. The ridge known as Stafford Heights, on the eastern bank of the Rappahannock, dominates Fredericksburg and provided a good location for the Union artillery commander, Brigadier General Henry J. Hunt, to mass his batteries. The heights also masked the location of Burnside's men from Confederate observers in Fredericksburg.

At the contested crossing point, the Rappahannock would require a bridge that was about 145yd long if the abutments are included. From the Rappahannock, the ground rises gently to Sophia Street where the riverfront houses were situated.

Besides being multilevel, some of these houses had cellars with windows facing the river.

The night of December 10/11 was cold, dark, and foggy. The fog limited visibility and Confederate pickets could not see across the river. The sound carried, however, and betrayed the Union engineers' activity. The fog would not lift until the morning and by that time it was too late for the engineers to remove the pontoons and start afresh. With the arrival of daylight, it became even more hazardous for any Union soldier who attempted to work on the bridges. It also meant that Union artillery positioned along Stafford Heights could bombard Fredericksburg.

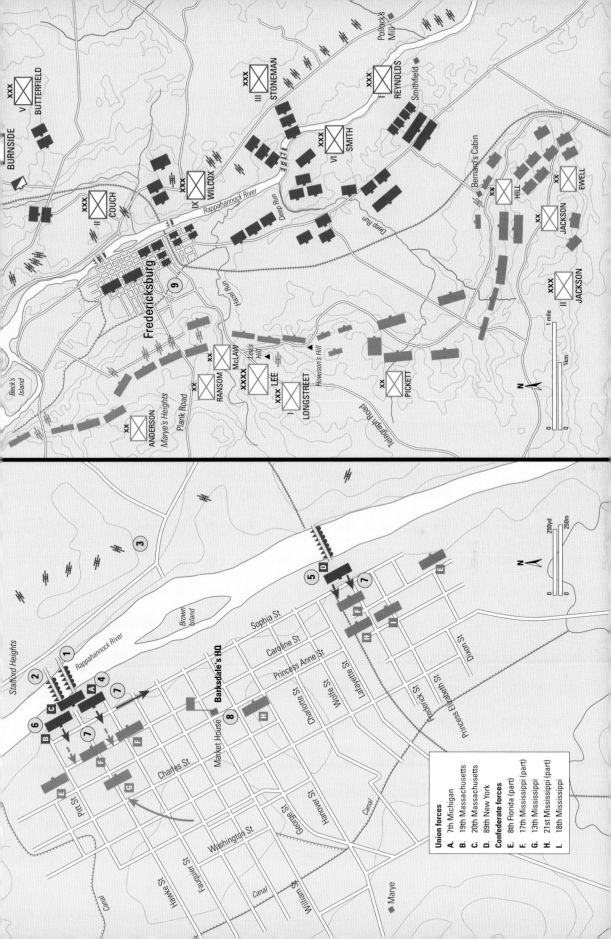

Right map (overview):

BURNSIDE

XXX V BUTTERFIELD

XXX III STONEMAN

XXX VI SMITH

XXX REYNOLDS

Pollock's Mill

Smithfield

XXX II COUCH

XXX IX WILCOX

Rappahannock River

Deep Run

Deep Run

Bernard's Cabin

XX HILL

XX EWELL

XX JACKSON

FREDERICKSBURG

9

Hazel Run

Beck's Island

Marye's Heights

Plank Road

XX ANDERSON

XX RANSOM

McLAW

XXXX LEE

Zoan's Hill

Howison's Hill

XXX I LONGSTREET

Telegraph Road

XX PICKETT

XXX II JACKSON

N

1 mile
1km

Left map (Fredericksburg town):

Stafford Heights

6

2

1

Rappahannock River

Brown Island

C

B

A

4

7

E

7

F

G

Barksdale's HQ

3

5

D

7

F

F

H

E

Sophia St

Caroline St

Princess Anne St

Charlotte St

Wolfe St

Lafayette St

Princess Elizabeth St

Frederick St

Dixon St

Market House

8

H

Charles St

Hanover St

George St

Canal

Washington St

Canal

Hawke St

Fauquier St

Canal

William St

Marye

N

250yd
250m

Union forces
A. 7th Michigan
B. 19th Massachusetts
C. 20th Massachusetts
D. 89th New York

Confederate forces
E. 8th Florida (part)
F. 17th Mississippi (part)
G. 13th Mississippi
H. 21st Mississippi (part)
I. 18th Mississippi

INTO COMBAT

At 0430hrs on December 11, when the Union engineers were halfway finished their bridge-building work and too committed to pull back, Confederate artillerymen of Read's Battery fired to signal to Barksdale that he should commence hostilities. Like a scythe, the Confederate sharpshooters' fire cut down the Union engineers, with the survivors fleeing. Burnside retaliated by bombarding Fredericksburg. Over 100 Union artillery pieces along with skirmishers from two infantry regiments and the 1st Andrew Sharpshooters fired at the smoke emanating from the Confederates' small arms. Major General Lafayette McLaws remarked on the weight of Union fire inflicted on the defenders (McLaws 1995: 87), noting the combination of bursting shells, noise, smoke, and flying debris engulfing the Confederate positions. Even under such a bombardment, the defenders – led by Lieutenant Colonel John C. Fiser, 17th Mississippi Infantry, and composed of that regiment plus the ten sharpshooters from the 13th Mississippi Infantry and three companies of the 18th Mississippi – remained at their posts. During the bombardment, the Confederates hid in the relative safety of house cellars. When the Union artillery fire lifted and the engineers rushed out to finish the bridges, the Confederates renewed their fire and drove them back again. An exasperated Captain Thomas W. Osborn, 1st New York Light Artillery (1st Division, IX Corps), could not understand why Sumner had opted to place the bridges so close to Fredericksburg, exposing the builders to fire from emplaced enemy sharpshooter fire (Crumb & Dhalle 1993: 92). It seemed obvious to Osborn that it would have been better to have bridged the Rappahannock farther north or south of the city, at locations where the defenders would have lacked cover.

Union artillery lined the heights above the Rappahannock River and dominated Fredericksburg. The town and its c.5,000 inhabitants successfully avoided the Civil War until the arrival of the Army of the Potomac. (Library of Congress)

A Union artillery battery shells Fredericksburg during the battle. The Union artillery deployed 147 guns of different types on Stafford Heights. (The Print Collector/ Print Collector/Getty Images)

Once again Burnside ordered the artillery and sharpshooters to silence the Confederate sharpshooters. When they thought the Confederates were silenced, the engineers returned to their bridge-building work with the same result. This was repeated several times until an amphibious assault was ordered. The 7th Michigan, 19th Massachusetts, and 89th New York Volunteer

Confederates identified as Barksdale's Mississippians are pictured on Fredericksburg's demolished railroad bridge. The photographer, Captain Andrew J. Russell of the United States Military Railroads, captured a fleeting moment of civility during a fratricidal civil war. None of the soldiers here is armed and the clarity of the image shows not only that they were aware that they were being photographed, but that they were willing to cooperate by remaining still for the photographer. In the distant background are the Wills Hill cemetery and Marye's Heights. (© CORBIS/ Corbis via Getty Images)

Sharpshooters at the forefront of battle

On the cold and foggy morning of December 11, 1862, Union pontoniers attempting to bridge the Rappahannock were driven back by Confederate sharpshooters. The bombardment undertaken by Union artillery along Stafford Heights only temporarily silenced the Confederate sharpshooters. When the pontoniers resumed working, the Confederate sharpshooters drove them back again. This cycle repeated itself throughout the morning. Finally, the 7th Michigan, 19th Massachusetts, and 1st Andrew Sharpshooters were ordered forward to suppress the Confederates. Their faster-loading breechloading Sharps rifles or accurate target rifles offered the Union sharpshooters no advantage. Exploding artillery shells and smoke from

Fredericksburg's burning buildings hindered their ability to suppress the Confederate sharpshooters and limited them to aiming, with indifferent results, at the sulfurous white smoke that belched from Confederate rifles.

While the Andrew Sharpshooters take advantage of the cover offered by some trees, one carelessly exposed Union soldier is falling back after being struck by a Minié ball. The pontoniers can be seen vainly attempting to finish their bridge. They would not be finished until an amphibious infantry assault by the 7th Michigan and the 19th Massachusetts secured a foothold on the riverbank and drove the Confederates from the waterfront.

Infantry boarded the pontoons and under covering fire of the Union artillery and sharpshooters, crossed the Rappahannock. Private Englis, serving with the 89th New York, did not give himself or his comrades much of a chance when his regiment was ordered to climb into the boats at about 1700hrs (Patch 2001: 59). McLaws, citing 1630hrs as the time when the Union boats set off, described how the weight of Union fire impeded his men's efforts to prevent the amphibious landing (McLaws 1995: 86–88).

Barksdale's men had accomplished their mission of delaying the crossing of the Rappahannock. At 1600hrs, when Longstreet had completed all his preparations for the battle, he ordered Barksdale to withdraw from Fredericksburg. Captain Osborn lamented the ineffectiveness of the shelling, and asserted that the amphibious operation should have occurred at sunrise rather than sunset (Crumb & Dhalle 1993: 93).

While ordered to retire, Barksdale's men engaged in intense street fighting for the town, fueled in one case by an intense rivalry between Harvard classmates leading units on opposing sides. Sergeant Joseph E. Hodgkins, 19th Massachusetts, remembered how his unit formed up on the riverbank before deploying as skirmishers and moving into the streets of Fredericksburg (Turion 1994: 16). As the men of Hodgkins' company advanced along the street they were hit by rifle fire from Confederates located in the buildings. Even after Hodgkins' party took shelter behind a fence, they were forced by the weight of the Confederate fire to retreat to the water's edge. Second Lieutenant John G.B. Adams of the same regiment had a similar experience:

As soon as the boats touched the shore we formed by companies, and, without waiting for regimental formation, charged up the street, on reaching the main street we found that the fire came from houses in front and rear. Company B lost ten men out of thirty in less than five minutes. Other companies suffered nearly the same. We were forced to fall back to the river, deploy as skirmishers, and reach the main street through the yard and houses. As we fell back we left one of our men wounded in the street; his name was Redding, of Company D, and when we again reached

the street we found him dead – the rebels having bayoneted him in several places. (Adams 1899: 50)

The 20th Massachusetts Volunteer Infantry formed itself and stormed up Hawke Street with disastrous results. Among the waiting Confederates of the 13th Mississippi was Private William L. Davis:

> One Yankee reg't formed a pretty line and was advancing up a street – a little before dark, our boys who were laying on the ground on the next street, quickly arose and poured a deadly volley into their midst causing the greatest confusion. The Yankee officer cried to his men to charge the rebels. Our boys, one and all, cried out, "Come on!" (Davis 1862)

Private Josiah F. Murphey, 20th Massachusetts, was among the men who received the Confederate volley (Miller & Mooney 1994: 89). Murphey's company, 60 or so men strong, received devastating fire from the Confederate defenders and suffered some 40 casualties in the space of 50yd – the company's highest casualty rate of the war, in Murphey's view. In that short space of 50yd, the 20th Massachusetts lost 97 men and officers killed and wounded. Fighting became personal when Lieutenant Lane Brandon of the 21st Mississippi Infantry recognized his Harvard Law School classmate, Major Henry L. Abbott of the 20th Massachusetts. Refusing to retreat, Brandon counterattacked and drove Abbott back. Ordered to

Unable to silence the Confederate sharpshooters, the Union forces launched an amphibious assault to secure the waterfront. Here we see Union soldiers boarding pontoons upon which they crossed the Rappahannock River. (Library of Congress)

retreat again, Brandon had to be arrested before he would yield ground. Despite the staggering Union losses, enough momentum remained for the Massachusetts men to storm one block up Caroline Street then wheel left and right and clear Caroline Street of the Confederates. Fredericksburg was secured for the Union by the evening of December 11 and Burnside's army crossed into the town.

Rolling up the Confederates who did not receive word to withdraw, the Union forces spent the evening expanding the bridgehead. The next day, December 12, was mostly confined to artillery duels and preparation for the next phase of battle. West of Fredericksburg was Marye's Heights and beneath it along a sunken road stood a stone wall where much of Longstreet's Corps waited. Asked by Lee if his men could hold against an assault, Longstreet assured Lee that given sufficient ammunition, they would. Burnside's major assault would be conducted by Major General William B. Franklin's Left Grand Division, which was tasked with attacking "Stonewall" Jackson's line, seizing the military road, and rolling up the Confederate flank. Sumner's Right Grand Division would assault Marye's Heights and draw Confederate attention away from Franklin.

Franklin began deploying his men during the morning of December 13. Major General George G. Meade led off Franklin's attack with his 3d Division (I Corps), supported by Brigadier General John Gibbon's 2d Division to his right and Brigadier General Abner Doubleday's 1st Division to his left. Meade slowly fought his way forward and broke through. Gibbon's division became entangled in the fighting around the railroad embankment, however, and fell behind. Doubleday's division advanced against Major General J.E.B. Stuart's cavalry and after securing its position, stopped.

In the hour before midday, as Jackson's men advanced to push Meade back, Burnside ordered Sumner to launch his secondary attack. Brigadier General William H. French's 3d Division (II Corps) led Sumner's attack, which was driven back. Brigadier General Winfield S. Hancock's 1st Division fared no better and Brigadier General Oliver O. Howard's 2d Division, supported by Brigadier General Samuel D. Sturgis's 2d Division (IX Corps), was also driven back. Each Union advance was met with artillery and musketry which drove the advancing columns to the ground. Private Thomas H. Mann, 18th Massachusetts Volunteer Infantry, described his experience in the fourth Union attack (Hennessy 2000: 122). During the initial charge, Mann and another soldier, William Laird, got farther than their comrades, getting within 80ft of a stone wall manned by the defenders. Having discharged his own rifle only once – as he turned to come back – Mann was hit five or six times by spent bullets, with two rounds smashing his rifle and another penetrating his equipment, rations and overcoat; he concluded that he was lucky to escape with his life.

As told by one Confederate officer, Lieutenant William M. Owen of the Washington Artillery of New Orleans, the battle for Marye's Heights was not a one-sided affair (Owen 1995: 99). Once the Union sharpshooters obtained the range of the Confederate embrasures, artillerists began to fall: Corporal Francis D. Ruggles was mortally wounded, with five others wounded in short order. The mounting casualties meant that officers and men alike were required to crew the guns, with infantrymen providing assistance with

Defending Fredericksburg for the Confederacy, Brigadier General William Barksdale's Mississippi Brigade would keep the Union forces at bay for over 11 hours. Barksdale's first military experience came during the Mexican–American War. After Mississippi seceded on January 9, 1861, Barksdale resigned and accepted the position of adjutant general with the rank of brigadier general in the Mississippi Militia. On May 1, 1861 he accepted the colonelcy of the 13th Mississippi Infantry, a regiment which faced the 1st Andrew Sharpshooters at Edward's Ferry. According to Captain Saunders of the 1st Andrew Sharpshooters, Barksdale's regiment was routed, but in reality Barksdale had been ordered to make a demonstration before falling back to support the main Confederate attack at Ball's Bluff. At Malvern Hill (July 1, 1862), Barksdale assumed command of Brigadier General Richard Griffin's brigade and was promoted to brigadier general on August 12, 1862. His brigade helped capture Harper's Ferry for the Confederacy by storming Maryland Heights on September 12, 1862. The brigade's next battle was at Antietam/Sharpsburg, where Barksdale's men fought in the West Woods against Major General John Sedgwick's 2d Division in Major General Edwin V. Sumner's II Corps. (NARA)

repositioning the pieces after each shot. In the course of 4½ hours, Owen recalled, three men were killed and 24 wounded.

Also coming under fire was Confederate artillery commander Colonel Edward P. Alexander, who was required to move between artillery positions in the course of his duties (Gallagher 1989: 180). Alexander noted an especially troublesome group of Union sharpshooters located in a brick tanyard to the east of the Orange Plank Road. The Union marksmen had made loopholes in the brickwork, and gave particular attention to the spot where the Confederate line crossed the road. As the Confederates had not built a breastwork to protect those crossing the road, even a running man risked being shot as he moved across it.

Near dusk, Brigadier General Andrew A. Humphreys' 3d Division (V Corps) advanced over the prone bodies of the earlier columns that were pinned down before them. Humphreys afterward wrote of the formidable fire offered by Confederate troops manning the stone wall (Palfrey 2002: 172). During the Union advance, the troops in the column did not fire until the head of the column approached the wall; although the Union troops began to discharge their firearms, the column began to retire, despite the efforts of Humphreys, the brigade commander, Brigadier General Erastus B. Tyler, or the two generals' staff.

Supporting Humphreys' assault was Brigadier General George Sykes' 2d Division (V Corps); it too was stopped. Among the pinned-down Union soldiers of Sykes' division was Captain John W. Ames, 11th US Infantry (Ames 1995: 123–24). Ames noted that the Confederate fire was highly accurate and made it impossible for the Union troops to retire. Sergeant Read asked Ames whether he could take a shot at a Confederate artillery officer with a spyglass, standing with the batteries threatening the right flank of Ames' regiment. Keen to avoid bringing down artillery fire on his men's positions, Ames refused Read's request, and the Confederate artillerists continued to ignore the pinned Union soldiers.

The Confederate artillery officer was Colonel Edward P. Alexander, who stated in his private memoirs that he was the only Confederate officer with a spyglass at the battle. Alexander explained why he never fired on them and how he received satisfaction against the sharpshooter who had annoyed him (Gallagher 1989: 180–81). When Alexander visited Longstreet, that officer authorized the use of some scarce artillery shells to counter the Union sharpshooters in the tanyard. Alexander carefully sighted an artillery piece; the shell almost brushed the ground as it flew over the low hill, then hit and exploded. There was a cheer from the Confederate pickets and one soldier ran back to explain that the shell had struck close to the corner loophole, killing one sharpshooter and wounding others; no further shots were fired from the tanyard that day.

Longstreet's promise that Marye's Heights could be held for the Confederacy was kept. Of the 12,653 Union casualties, Longstreet estimated that 5,000 were from rifle fire alone. Confederate casualties amounted to 5,377. The climactic battle won for the Confederacy at Marye's Heights was made possible by Barksdale, his Mississippians, and their sharpshooters who played a vital role in holding the Union forces at the river bank for 16 hours, giving Longstreet valuable time to complete his dispositions for battle (Longstreet 1992: 316).

Vicksburg

May 18–July 4, 1863

BACKGROUND TO BATTLE

Vicksburg, Mississippi, was a key commercial center on the Mississippi River through which cattle, materiel, and men moved from the Trans-Mississippi region to the rest of the Confederacy. Its capture along with the capture of Port Hudson, Louisiana, would open the river for Union traffic to the Gulf of Mexico and sever the Trans-Mississippi from the rest of the Confederacy.

Lieutenant General John C. Pemberton, commanding the Department of Mississippi and Eastern Louisiana, was responsible for defending Vicksburg and its environs. Pemberton's army included four divisions, commanded by Major General Carter L. Stevenson, Major General John H. Forney, Major General Martin L. Smith, and Major General John S. Bowen. The only Confederate sharpshooter unit present was the 12th Arkansas Battalion Sharpshooters, part of Bowen's Division. Many of Pemberton's c.29,500 men were hospitalized due to wounds or sickness.

Commanding the Union ground forces was Major General Ulysses S. Grant, who had attempted to capture Vicksburg four times already (December 1862–March 1863). To many, Grant appeared to be one of a succession of failed Union generals, and the sword of Damocles hung over him as he embarked upon his fifth campaign to take the city. In late March 1862, in a bold move that severed his communication with Washington, DC, Grant marched his army along the west bank of the Mississippi to a point below Vicksburg so as to approach it from the south. Rear Admiral David D. Porter of the Union Navy escorted Grant's supply barges past Vicksburg and rendezvoused with him.

In a brilliant campaign, Grant fought five battles in quick succession – Port Gibson (May 1), Raymond (May 12), Jackson (May 14), Champion

This depiction of life in the Union trenches at Vicksburg shows the numerous tents, shanties or shebangs that were used as shelters by the soldiers of Brigadier General Mortimer D. Leggett's 1st Brigade, Major General John A. Logan's 3d Division of Major General James B. McPherson's XVII Corps. The steep ravines described by Grant in his memoirs can be seen near the center of the image. In the distant background is the Shirley House (White House), which fronted the Jackson Road. Late spring and summer months in Vicksburg are very hot. During the siege, only four days of rain were recorded (May 22, May 23, June 10, and June 24) and the scarcity of water was a concern to both sides. With water being in great demand and short supply, sanitation must have been difficult for both belligerents. Men suffered from heatstroke or became ill because of poor hygiene. As the siege wore on, food became scarce for the Confederates, who subsisted on reduced rations. (Buyenlarge/Getty Images)

Hill (May 16), and Big Black River Bridge (May 17) – defeating each Confederate force in succession and driving away any relief effort that threatened him. He compelled the surviving Confederate forces to fall back into Vicksburg. During the ensuing siege of the city, Grant commanded three corps – Major General John A. McClernand's XIII Corps, Major General William T. Sherman's XV Corps, and Major General James B. McPherson's XVII Corps – that deployed eight divisions at the outset, rising to ten by early July.

The loess soil hills that dominated and protected Vicksburg from its landward side proved to be easy to dig; the undisturbed or sculpted soil held its form rather well, resulting in stable trench walls and mine tunnels that did not require much shoring up. Grant described the terrain surrounding Vicksburg:

> The ground about Vicksburg is admirable for defence. On the north it is about two hundred feet above the Mississippi River at the highest point and very much cut up by the washing rains; the ravines were grown up with cane and underbrush, while the sides and tops were covered with a dense forest. Farther south the ground flattens out somewhat, and was in cultivation. But here, too, it was cut up by ravines and small streams. The enemy's line of defence followed the crest of a ridge from the river north of the city eastward, then southerly around to the Jackson road, full three miles back of the city; thence in a southwesterly direction to the river. Deep ravines of the description given lay in front of these defences. As there is a succession of gullies, cut out by rains along the side of the ridge, the line was necessarily very irregular. To follow each of these spurs with intrenchments, so as to command the slopes on either side, would have lengthened their line very much. Generally therefore, or in many places, their line would run from near the head of one gully nearly straight to the head of another, and an outer work triangular in shape, generally open in the rear, was thrown up on the point; with a few men in this outer work they commanded the approaches to the main line completely. (Grant 1885: 535–36)

The siege of Vicksburg, May 19–July 4, 1863

MAP KEY

1 May 19–23: On May 19, a day after the arrival of his army before Vicksburg, Major General Ulysses S. Grant calculates that the Confederates are demoralized and attempts to storm Vicksburg by *coup de main*; he is driven back with 942 Union casualties. On May 22, Grant tries a more organized assault that is preceded by a heavy artillery bombardment. He suffers 502 killed, 2,550 wounded, and 147 captured. On May 23, the siege begins, with Union positions up to 800yd from the Confederate defenses.

2 June 8: Union forces use a cotton-clad railcar as a sap roller against the 3d Louisiana Redan; the railcar is destroyed by incendiary bullets a day later.

3 June 9: Lieutenant Henry C. "Coonskin" Foster's sniper tower is completed.

4 June 17: Colonel Isham W. Garrott, 20th Alabama Infantry, is aiming a rifle while defending the Square Fort when he is shot through the heart by a Union sharpshooter stationed in a tree.

5 June 21: Union forces open a parallel within 60yd of the 27th Louisiana Lunette. On June 22, Union sharpshooters kill or wound every field officer of the 27th Louisiana Infantry.

6 June 22: A mine is started beneath the 3d Louisiana Redan. The mine is sprung on June 25, but not before the Confederates withdraw from the redan, having built a traverse behind it which enables them to defeat the Union assault.

7 June 27: Confederate Brigadier General Martin E. Green is killed by a Union sharpshooter.

8 June 28: Union forces start a new mine to the north of the old one. By June 30, all Union approaches are between 5yd and 120yd of the Confederate perimeter; Grant plans an all-out assault for July 6. On July 1, Union forces spring the second mine at the 3d Louisiana Redan, but there is no follow-up attack.

9 July 2: Confederate forces explode a countermine on a Union sap against Railroad Redoubt.

10 July 3: White flags wave over the Confederate lines. Pemberton meets with Grant and in the evening they come to terms. Vicksburg capitulates on July 4.

Battlefield environment

The 8 miles of Confederate defensive lines were strengthened by nine strongpoints. Anchoring the Confederate line in the north was Fort Hill, controlling the Valley Road that parallels the Yazoo River. Running east along the ridge from Fort Hill was Graveyard Road (Cemetery Road) and guarding the midpoint of the ridge was the 27th Louisiana Lunette. From the lunette the line ran east a short distance to the Stockade Redan, at which point the defenses along with the ridge turned south. While interrupted by a gully, the ridge continued to the Vicksburg–Jackson Road that led to the state capitol, Jackson. North of and protecting the Jackson Road was the 3d Louisiana Redan. Following the ridge south was the 2d Texas Lunette that guarded the Baldwin Ferry Road. Next in line, guarding

the Vicksburg & Jackson Railroad, was the Railroad Redoubt; it was also the dividing line between Major General James B. McPherson's XVII Corps and Major General Edward O.C. Ord's XIII Corps. The Square Fort lay a half-mile south; 1 mile south of that was the Salient Work, commanding the Hall's Ferry Road. Anchoring the Southern defenses 1¾ miles away from the Salient Work was the South Fort that guarded the Warrenton Road.

Grant's army constructed 15 miles of siege works and 13 saps, of which only four were viable: those along the Graveyard Road toward the Stockade Redan, at the Jackson road, the Baldwin Ferry Road, and the Railroad Redoubt.

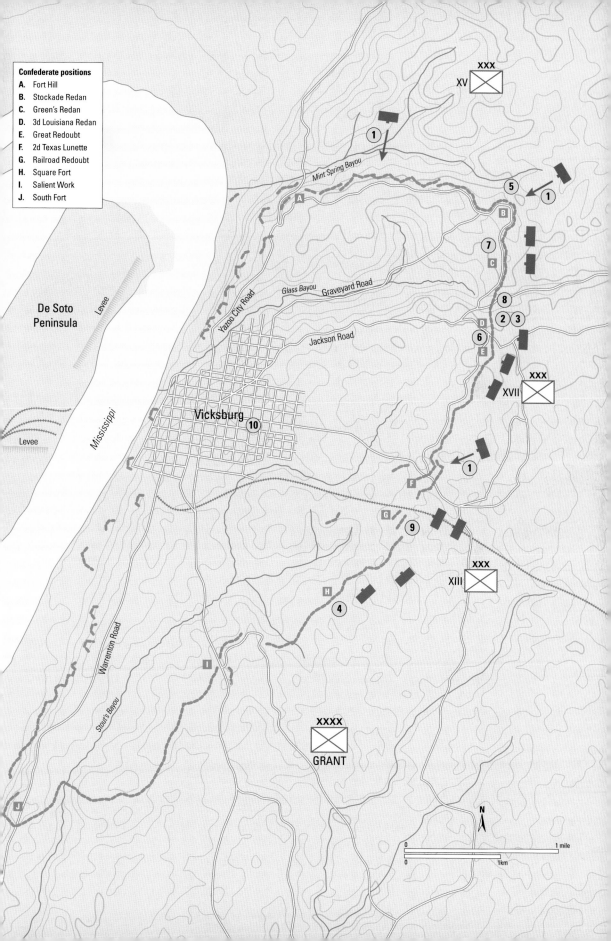

Confederate positions

A. Fort Hill
B. Stockade Redan
C. Green's Redan
D. 3d Louisiana Redan
E. Great Redoubt
F. 2d Texas Lunette
G. Railroad Redoubt
H. Square Fort
I. Salient Work
J. South Fort

De Soto
Peninsula

Levee

Levee

Mississippi

Vicksburg

Yazoo City Road

Glass Bayou

Graveyard Road

Jackson Road

Mint Spring Bayou

Warrenton Road

Stout's Bayou

GRANT

N

0   1 mile

0   1km

INTO COMBAT

During the Civil War, sieges were conducted in the traditional manner. A trench, called a parallel, was dug that paralleled the defenders' lines. Embrasures were built along the trench in which artillery was emplaced to suppress the defenders' artillery. Once a parallel was finished, zigzag approaches were dug to shield the engineers as they dug their way forward. To protect the engineers from incoming fire, a huge woven wicker-and-wood basket called a sap roller, 8ft long and 4ft in diameter and filled with sticks, was pushed ahead of them by means of hooks and levers. Their flanks were protected by gabions, open-ended wicker baskets filled with dirt after they were placed in position, that lined the top of the trench. While the sap roller and gabion were impervious to small-arms fire, they did little to stop artillery. When a zigzag approach reached close enough, another parallel was started and more artillery brought up to suppress the defenders. The process was repeated until the besieger was close enough to storm the fortification in one orchestrated rush that minimized casualties. The final fight would be over very quickly, and it was not unusual for a defender to capitulate or evacuate before the assault.

On May 19, Pemberton's forces easily repulsed Grant's first attempt to take Vicksburg by storm. Two days later, Grant's artillery began to demolish the cotton-bale breastworks that protected the Confederates from sharpshooter fire. This exposed the Confederate artillerymen, and one Confederate battery had five men attempting to light a fuze shot down in succession. Grant's second attack was launched on May 22, but that too was repulsed. Conscious of the casualties suffered during these actions, Grant settled upon a siege, digging siege lines to invest Vicksburg along the riverbank both north and south of the city. A total of 89 artillery batteries would be dug in to bombard the Confederates. As the belligerents settled down, the sharpshooting intensified.

Within two weeks Grant's men began gaining the upper hand. The 76th Ohio Volunteer Infantry was stationed adjacent to the eastern bank of the Mississippi. Captain Richard W. Burt of that regiment described the siege:

> This is the 13th day of the siege [May 30] and the Rebels still hold the city … [W]e have them entirely surrounded, our army being entrenched on all the surrounding hills, from 200 to 1,000 yards from their line of forts and rifle pits, and our gunboats on the river … Our regiment has occupied this position since the second day of the siege, and has been practicing sharpshooting at the Rebels all the time, until they hardly dare to raise their heads above the rifle pits. Their artillery seems to be silenced, as they have fired only a few shots for several days along the line as far as we can see to the left. We have two 30-pounder Parrots and 6 6-pounders on the hill we occupy, from which we can give their works an enfilading fire. (Burt 1863)

The Confederates had made the mistake of entrenching on the ridgeline and anyone standing up to look was silhouetted against the skyline. First Lieutenant Charles D. Miller, adjutant of the 76th Ohio, recalled how the Confederates killed one soldier of his regiment, Lieutenant Charles Luther of

Born in Pennsylvania to a Quaker family in 1814, John C. Pemberton graduated from West Point's class of 1837 and was commissioned an engineer. Pemberton developed southern sympathies and later married Martha Thompson, a Virginian. When war broke out, Pemberton offered his services to the Confederacy and was appointed as brigadier general commanding the Department of South Carolina, Georgia, and Florida. His attempt to raise sharpshooter battalions in South Carolina was a dismal failure, but he was more successful with the battalions raised in Georgia. He was promoted to major general (January 14, 1862) and upon being transferred to the Department of Mississippi and Eastern Louisiana, to lieutenant general (October 10, 1862), making the defense of Vicksburg and its environs his responsibility. Placed in command of Vicksburg, he benefited from the work undertaken by his predecessor, Brigadier General Martin L. Smith, to fortify the city, but insufficient food, inadequate medicine, and the lack of a relief force would doom Pemberton and his men to capture. (Library of Congress)

Company E, who was shot in the head around 1700hrs on May 24 (Bennett & Tillery 2004: 97). Just before Luther was killed, Miller had been observing the trajectory of Union artillery fire, and called his fellow officer over to see the shot moving toward the Confederate positions; a moment after he took Miller's place, Luther was hit. Miller could not resist borrowing a Springfield rifle-musket and shooting back from the rifle pits (Bennett & Tillery 2004: 106). Wishing to target a Confederate sharpshooter, the soldier next to Miller made ready to fire; before he could pull the trigger, a bullet hit him in the head, killing him.

Among the strongpoints in the Confederate lines was the 3d Louisiana Redan. For the most part, the occupants of this strongpoint and the adjacent Confederate units silenced the besieging artillery and compelled the Union gunners to resort to using rope curtains and merlons to protect themselves. The Union commanders understood that these strongpoints had to be captured. Accordingly, Union forces made an attempt to push a cotton-clad railcar ahead of themselves. It served successfully as a sap roller, stopping any small-arms fire, until during the evening of June 9, Lieutenant W.M. Washburn, 3d Louisiana Infantry, filled the cavity of a Minié ball with turpentine-soaked cotton and fired it into the railcar; after a while, it began smoldering (Bearss 1998: 247–48). Other Confederates quickly mimicked Washburn's action and fired smoldering Minié balls into the railcar, while others drove away the Union soldiers who attempted to extinguish the flames. Predictably, the railcar burned down and that threat was removed.

Among the Union soldiers was Lieutenant Henry C. Foster, serving in Company B, 23d Indiana Volunteer Infantry. Reputed to be the best shot in Grant's army, he was nicknamed "Coonskin" Foster for the racoonskin cap he wore in lieu of the regulation headgear. Lieutenant Colonel Andrew Hickenlooper, the XVIII Corps chief of staff, sent back an account of Foster's activities that was published in a local newspaper (Hickenlooper 1995: 541). Under cover of darkness, Foster moved toward the Confederate lines and made himself a hide below ground. His practice was to remain in the burrow for days at a time, observing the enemy. Taking advantage of the wreckage of the Vicksburg & Jackson Railroad, Foster constructed a tower over the course of several nights. Its height allowed Foster to see and target Confederate personnel beyond the parapets. With the Confederate artillery having been silenced and only small arms available, the defenders could not damage the tower.

Foster personally profited from the tower too, charging curious soldiers a quarter to have a look from the structure. Presumably he did not charge his commanding officer, Major General Grant, for an opportunity to study the Confederate lines from it. While Grant was surveying the Confederate defenses with field glasses, one rebel spotted him and used obscenities when he told Grant not to expose himself. A Confederate captain chastised the soldier for speaking offensively to an officer; albeit a Yankee one.

To counter the Confederate sharpshooters at the 3d Louisiana Redan, the Union soldiers used sandbags to build their loopholes and from behind them killed or wounded every field officer from the 27th Louisiana Infantry on June 22. In desperation, the Confederates made a dummy which they

The commanding general of the Union forces besieging Vicksburg, Ulysses S. Grant, depicted here in June 1864, earned two brevets in the Mexican–American War but resigned from the Army in July 1854. With war's outbreak, Grant received an appointment as colonel of the 21st Illinois Volunteer Infantry. He soon received his brigadier general's star and in cooperation with Rear Admiral David D. Porter of the Union Navy, captured Forts Henry and Donelson in Tennessee in February 1862. Surprised and pushed back at the battle of Shiloh on April 6, he fought again the next day and regained all the lost ground, forcing the Confederates to fall back to Corinth, Mississippi. He showed his mettle as a fighting general who fought five battles in 17 days before bottling up the Confederates at Vicksburg. While Grant was primarily a strategist who did not think in tactical terms, he did appreciate the utility of sharpshooting. His sharpshooters would successfully suppress the Confederate defenders at Vicksburg and forced Pemberton's infantry to keep their heads down. He noted the various defensive means (sandbags, loopholes, headlogs) the Union sharpshooters employed at Vicksburg to protect themselves against enemy sharpshooters (Grant 1885: 538). (Library of Congress)

Henry C. Foster

On July 27, 1861, Sergeant Henry C. Foster mustered in at Clark County in Company B, 23d Indiana Volunteer Infantry. He was promoted to lieutenant before Shiloh and was involved in the battles leading up to Vicksburg. It was at Vicksburg that Foster earned notoriety as a sharpshooter. Foregoing the regulation kepi or slouch hat, Foster adopted a racoonskin cap and the moniker, "Coonskin" Foster. He would snipe at unwary Confederates who exposed themselves. Taking several days' provisions with him, Foster once crept out at night, burrowed into the ground and dug a peephole through which he shot Confederates. With the help of men from Companies B and E, Foster built a log cabin-style tower that overlooked the Confederate parapets. As Confederate artillery had been silenced, he sniped at them through small chinks between the logs with little fear of retaliation.

After Vicksburg's capture, Foster was promoted to first lieutenant and given a 20-day meritorious leave. He was captured at Kennesaw Mountain and incarcerated at Camp Asylum, South Carolina. He escaped (February 14–15) while being transferred to another prison and rejoined Sherman's army. Foster mustered out of service on July 23, 1865, and moved to Chicago in 1887.

propped over their parapet. When fired upon, the Confederates would lower the dummy as if it had jumped down. They would wait a while, prop it back up then cry out, "Try again, will you, Mr. Yankee?" It took a while before the Union soldiers discovered that they had been duped.

Exposing oneself became hazardous and Union engineer Lieutenant Peter C. Haines found a clever method to survey the Confederate line: "I made a novel reconnaissance of the enemy's ditch this morning, by means of a mirror attached to a pole being raised above the sap roller, and a little to the rear, and then inclined forward. A perfect view of the ditch was by this means obtainable" (OR, Series I, Vol. XXIV, Part 2: 185). A half-century later, periscopes were common equipment in the trenches of World War I. Using a similar concept, Sergeant William R. Eddington, Company A, 97th Illinois Volunteer Infantry, wrote home revealing how to shoot without exposing oneself (Eddington n.d.). He explained how he would sharpen one end of a small stick and split the other end, placing a looking glass in the split. With his rifle in an embrasure behind him and his thumb on the trigger, he would then sit with his back toward the Confederate positions and wait; when he spotted anything he would fire. Another man found a bent plow and dug it in, using it for his loophole. It saved him from counterfire several times. Eddington shared his post with two others; one man would rest while the other two remained alert – one to shoot and the other to reload. Such activities could be maintained for hours at a time.

Eddington also described discovering a Confederate sharpshooter. Investigating a newly dug trench, Eddington was nearly hit by an enemy bullet. When he ventured into the same area again, a second bullet followed the first, alerting him to the presence of a Confederate sharpshooter. Spotting a pile of fresh dirt, denoting the recent construction of a rifle pit, Eddington returned to his post and asked his comrades to aim at the dirt pile. Eddington then raised a cap on his rifle, prompting the enemy marksman to fire at it; the Union sharpshooters then opened fire and silenced the Confederate.

At Green's Redan, named after Brigadier General Martin E. Green whose brigade held it, Captain John S. Bell of the 12th Arkansas Battalion

Charles Ingram

Born November 16, 1838 in Prince Edward County, Virginia, Charles Ingram relocated with his family to Keytesville, Missouri, and then to Bonham, Texas, where he became a farmer. At war's outbreak, Ingram enlisted in the 3d Missouri Infantry and fought at Carthage, Lexington, Wilson's Creek, Pea Ridge, Corinth, Champion Hill, and Big Black before his unit was forced to retreat to Vicksburg. He was captured on July 4, 1863, when Pemberton surrendered Vicksburg to Grant.

Paroled after Vicksburg, Ingram served in Cleburne's Division where he was issued a Whitworth rifle (serial number C-334) that he carried during the Atlanta Campaign (May–September 1864). Ingram also fought at Peach Tree Creek, Franklin, Nashville, and after General John B. Hood's retreat, was at Fort Blakely. When Mobile surrendered on April 12, 1865, Ingram fled west to join General Edmund K. Smith. After crossing the Mississippi River, Ingram learned of Smith's surrender. Post-war, Ingram married and became a merchant in the Choctaw Nation; he passed away in Durant, Oklahoma, on January 25, 1908. Ingram's Whitworth rifle is displayed at the 45th Infantry Division Museum in Oklahoma City, Oklahoma.

Sharpshooters assumed command of a portion of the redan on June 5. He relieved an unidentified major who gave him an orientation walk:

After showing me around and giving me information and precaution, he carried me to the right side of the fort and, pointing to a solitary pine tree on a knoll probably five hundred yards away and some forty feet to the first limb, informed me that every morning a Yankee sharpshooter would climb up in the forks of the tree, that he had killed one of his men and wounded several in the fort, that he had tried to dislodge him, but had not. Wishing me a pleasant(?) time, he marched his men out, and I took command. Next morning our adjutant, [First Lieutenant] John Dupuy, and I were making an inspection of the fort, when our friend in the tree promptly gave us to understand that he was ready for business by sending several bullets near our heads. I called several of my best shots over and had them try their hands on him, but all failed to hit him, he made it dangerous for a man to cross the fort for several days. Finally a little fellow named White came up and proposed to go out at night, crawl up close to the tree before day, hide under the treetops that had been felled to impede the Yankees in charging, and, as soon as it was light enough to shoot, pick off the Yankee in the tree. I told him that it was a desperate risk, as he would be several hundred yards inside the Yankee lines, but he only laughed and said he was a desperate man. I consented, and he left the fort about 3 a.m. At daylight, with a number of our men, I was watching the tree and had about concluded White had failed, when I saw a puff of smoke rise from the brush about fifty yards from the tree. The report of the rifle had not reached me when I saw the body of a man tumble like a squirrel out of the fork some fifty feet from the ground. All was quiet for some ten minutes, when we saw a squad of Yankees move toward the tree. They found their man dead all right, but seemed to be puzzled as to who killed him. We opened fire on them and they picked him up and left. When White returned to the fort that night, he reported that the man had climbed the tree before daylight, but it was too dark for him to see the sights on his gun, so he had to wait. After shooting he ran some distance and hid in a ravine, where he remained concealed in the brush all day. He saw the Yankees looking for him, and several times they were close to his hiding place. (Bell 1904: 446)

In an attempt to break the Confederate defenses, a mine was sprung beneath the 3d Louisiana Redan on June 25. While the explosion was spectacular, the Confederates repelled the follow-up assault by Major General John A. Logan's forces, inflicting heavy losses on the attackers, and the sought-after breach was never achieved. In the center background is "Coonskin's Tower"; the men at the loopholes are members of "Coonskin" Foster's detachment of sharpshooters. (Library of Congress)

The Union engineers tunneled underneath the 3d Louisiana Redan's protective ditch and soldiers of Major General John A. Logan's 3d Division (XVII Corps) mined the redan. Over 1 ton of black powder was placed beneath the redan. Five batteries of artillery would then fire upon the supporting Confederate positions. Foster had 100 picked marksmen who occupied a parallel that flanked the redan. When the mine was sprung, a brigade of Logan's men would rush in to capture it and break through to Vicksburg.

At about 1530hrs on June 25, the mine was sprung, sending men and debris in all directions; this was the signal for the Union artillery to open fire. Foster's men supported the attack by firing from loopholes at the Confederates. During an hour or so of fighting, a Union brigade gained a foothold but never penetrated the Confederate line (Winschel 1999: 58). As the Confederates were aware of the mining, they had taken the precaution of erecting a traverse across the redan's gorge. This sheltered the Confederates from the blast and when the Union infantry attacked, the Confederates met them with fierce resistance. Logan fed in fresh troops without appreciable gain. Grant conceded, "The breach was not sufficient to enable us to pass a column of attack through" (Grant 1885: 551). A second mine was started and blown on July 1. This time there was no follow-up attack as its only purpose was to destroy the redan.

Wounded before the 3d Louisiana Redan was blown, Green had himself released from the hospital and visited Green's Redan to check on the welfare of his men. His guide, Captain Bell, "warned him not to look through the

portholes until we fired a few shots to keep the Yankees down" (Bell 1904: 447). Brushing off Bell's suggestion, Green then stepped up to peer through a porthole. The result was predictable: "He failed to heed the warning, and at the second porthole through which he looked was shot and instantly killed" (Bell 1904: 447).

One innovation used by the Union forces to silence the Confederate sharpshooters was their homemade mortars. Lieutenant Peter C. Haines, Chief Engineer XIII Corps, describes them: "In the latter part of the siege the want of mortars was so severely felt that I gave the orders to have wooden mortars made, to be used with small charges of powder and light shells (6 and 12 pounds)" (OR, Series I, Vol. XXIV, Part 2: 182). The mortars were not invented by Haines; he had heard of them from other men serving in McPherson's XVII Corps:

I learned that General McPherson was using mortars made of trunks of trees (gum trees being the best) to throw 6 and 12 pound shells, and directed him to make some of these also, shrinking about three iron bands around the mortar. These mortars, which are said to work admirably for about 100 rounds, will

While defending Vicksburg, Brigadier General Martin E. Green was wounded (June 25) and hospitalized. Upon learning that the Union forces were becoming increasingly aggressive, Green had himself discharged from hospital (June 27) and resumed command of his brigade. While inspecting the defenses held by the 12th Arkansas Battalion Sharpshooters that day, Green was cautioned not to look through a loophole without first having the men fire some shots to suppress the Union sharpshooters. Exclaiming that the bullet that would kill him had not yet been molded, Green ignored the suggestion and was killed by a bullet that entered the loophole. (Public Domain)

be finished and stuck in the ground in the advance trenches, so that they will only have to throw shells about 50 or 75 yards. (OR, Series I, Vol. XXIV, Part 2: 186)

By July 3, Grant had numerous mines set and ready to be blown. His zigzag approaches were close enough that his men could storm the enemy fortifications with the minimum of exposure. With Confederate food supplies low, ammunition almost exhausted, and no relief in sight, Pemberton knew it was over. Of his 30,000 men, almost one-quarter (7,000) were hospitalized from malaria, dysentery, gangrene, and measles. Ominously, Pemberton also received a letter, signed "many troops," stating that further sacrifice was useless and hinting of mutiny if he did not surrender. Unable to break out to join Lieutenant General Joseph E. Johnston's relief army, Pemberton had no choice and raised the white flag at 1000hrs. In hopes of getting better terms, Pemberton sent Grant's old neighbor, Major General Bowen, to parlay with Grant; but Grant refused to meet Bowen and sent a note back that he would meet Pemberton at McPherson's line, just south of the 3d Louisiana Redan. Pemberton and his staff met Grant and his staff beneath a tree at 1500hrs. Grant denied any terms other than unconditional surrender with no honors of war to be accorded to the Confederates. After Grant offered to parole the Confederates, Pemberton consented, and Grant's men marched into Vicksburg on July 4 to accept his surrender.

After a 47-day siege, the Union banner flew over Vicksburg for the first time in two years. Its loss was a shock to the Confederacy. Wisely, rather than send the Confederates north to prisoner-of-war camps where they would have to be housed and fed, Grant paroled them instead, calculating that many would never fight again under the Confederate colors. Many did not. In capturing Vicksburg, Grant demonstrated his skill as a strategist, a tenacious fighter, and – most importantly – as a general who delivered victory. After receiving his parole and being exchanged on October 13, 1863, Pemberton returned to Virginia and resigned his commission on May 9, 1864. Humbly, three days later he accepted a commission as lieutenant colonel of artillery in command of Richmond's defenses.

Battery Wagner

July 19–September 6, 1863

BACKGROUND TO BATTLE

Charleston, South Carolina was viewed by many in the North as the hotbed of secession. From its environs the first shots had been fired that plunged the nation into war. In the wake of Gettysburg (July 3, 1863) and the Union capture of Vicksburg (July 4), Charleston's fall would be symbolic of Union victory. Fort Sumter commanded the entrance to Charleston Harbor and securing its "back door" were the Confederate forts on Morris Island. Commanding the Confederates at Charleston at the beginning of July 1863 was Lieutenant General Pierre Gustave Toutant Beauregard, the Confederacy's first general and a Southern hero for firing on Fort Sumter in April 1861. Brigadier General Roswell S. Ripley's 1st District included five subdivisions, with Brigadier General Johnson Hagood's 1st Subdivision garrisoning James Island and Brigadier General Thomas L. Clingman's 3d Subdivision holding Morris Island.

Having made a name for himself in April 1862 by conquering Fort Pulaski in Georgia, Brigadier General Quincy A. Gillmore replaced Major General David Hunter as commander of the Department of the South in June that year. In late May Gillmore was summoned to Washington, DC, where he outlined his four-part plan to capture Charleston. First, he would land troops on Morris Island. Second, his men would capture Battery Wagner and Battery Gregg on Morris Island. Third, Fort Sumter would be reduced and captured. Finally, with Fort Sumter taken, ships of the Union Navy would sail into Charleston Bay, bombard the city, and help capture Charleston.

On July 10, Gillmore executed the first part of his plan. Covered by artillery and three scoped rifle-equipped soldiers of Company K, 7th Connecticut Volunteer Infantry, Union forces landed on Morris Island and its Light House

Inlet. Fierce fighting ensued before the Union forces captured the rifle pits and artillery posted on the southern part of Morris Island. When the Union forces attempted to storm Battery Wagner the next day, they were supported by sharpshooters. Among the Confederate casualties was Captain Paul H. Waring, who was struck by a bullet when he was outside the tent of Battery Wagner's commanding officer, Brigadier General William B. Taliaferro. The bullet passed completely through the side of Waring's body and was probably fired from the roof of the Beacon House from where the Union sharpshooters with scope-equipped target rifles operated, more than 1,600yd away from Waring's position.

Gillmore's attempted *coup de main* on July 11 was repulsed by Battery Wagner's garrison. On July 18, the Union forces attacked again, supported by fire from the Union Navy blockading squadron, Union Army artillery batteries, five Billinghurst Requa Battery guns, and six sharpshooters with target rifles under the leadership of Captain James M. Nichols, 48th New York Infantry. Led by the 54th Massachusetts Volunteer Infantry, the Union's premier African-American regiment, the attack was again repulsed. The 54th Massachusetts alone suffered 42 percent casualties including its colonel, Robert G. Shaw; in total, the Union suffered 1,515 casualties (246 killed, 880 wounded, and 389 missing) while the Confederates incurred only 222 (48 killed, 162 wounded, and 5 missing, plus seven others whose fate is

As one of the original Union batteries on Morris Island, Battery Hays participated in the July 18 bombardment of Battery Wagner that preceded the ill-fated infantry assault. The bombardment was composed of a left wing armed with seven 30-pdr Parrott rifles and a right wing that had two pairs of 20-pdr Parrott rifles, two 30-pdrs, and an 8in Parrott rifle that stood apart from the rest. While Parrott rifles were deadly accurate, their elevating screws tended to break – and worse, the rifles themselves could burst. Gillmore reported 24 Parrott rifles blowing up, including the famous "Swamp Angel." (© CORBIS/Corbis via Getty Images)

This image shows the lighthouse keeper's quarters (the Beacon House) that the Confederates neglected to tear down when they fortified Morris Island; the Beacon House was initially used by Union sharpshooters to pick off Confederates at Battery Wagner. During the July 11 assault, Captain Paul H. Waring died after being shot through the side. Union engineers used wood salvaged from the Beacon House to build their trenches. (Library of Congress)

unknown). Reluctant to risk another assault, Gillmore elected to use siege tactics to capture Battery Wagner. While tediously slow and labor-intensive, such methods reduced Union casualties.

MAP KEY

1 July 19: Union forces commence work on the first parallel, completed on July 23; a second parallel is started 600yd in front of the first parallel. On July 25, Confederate sharpshooters arrive and begin targeting the Union engineers. On July 31, to protect them from sharpshooting, the Union artillery crews receive circular rope mantlets for their guns, but these prove to be ineffective against the Whitworth bolt.

2 August 9: The second parallel is completed and a third parallel is ordered 330yd in front of it. A flying sap is used to protect the Union engineers. On August 10, Brigadier General Quincy A. Gillmore admits that Union progress has been almost completely stopped by the Confederate sharpshooters. On August 13, Captain Richard Ela's Union sharpshooters join the fight.

3 August 16: The Union land batteries and blockading squadron conduct an intense bombardment to suppress the Confederate sharpshooters. Despite this, sharpshooters from both sides engage in brisk fire.

4 August 21: The third parallel is finished and a fourth parallel is started. On August 22, Parrott rifles are trained on sandbags where Confederate sharpshooters are known to operate.

5 August 26: Confederate rifle pits on the sand ridge are captured and immediately converted to a fifth parallel. Union forces are now roughly 200yd from Battery Wagner.

6 September 6: Union forces conduct an extensive bombardment of Battery Wagner and the Union sap is pushed to Battery Wagner's ditch. On September 6–7, Battery Wagner and Battery Gregg are abandoned by the Confederates.

Battlefield environment

Morris Island, a crystalline sand island situated on Charleston Bay. In 1863 it lay 1,390yd south of Fort Sumter; 3¾ miles long, its width varied from 25yd to 1,000yd. In the antebellum era, it was a quarantine station and acquired the nickname of "Coffin Island" from the quarantined people who were interred there. Native grasses and plants abound on Morris Island, along with a few trees. As the siege took place during the summer months of 1863, the weather was very hot. There was some rainfall and even a storm during the siege, but most soldiers complained of the heat.

To assist navigation, a lighthouse was constructed on the southern end of Morris Island and the Beacon House was built to house the lighthouse keeper and his family. On the northern tip of the island, about 1,390yd south of Fort Sumter, stood Battery Gregg, which guarded Fort Sumter's vulnerable southern face, known as "the Gorge." Protecting Battery Gregg from a northward thrust on Morris Island itself was Battery Wagner, built after Morris Island's vulnerability was revealed during the battle of Secessionville on June 16, 1862.

Battery Wagner was 5,500yd from the southern tip of Morris Island and 2,600yd from Fort Sumter. Situated on top of a sand ridge, Battery Wagner was 800ft long on its southern-facing land face and 300ft long on its sea face. The land face had embrasures for nine guns that concentrated on the island's neck, a narrow 25yd-wide killing zone. Its sea face had a 10in Columbiad cannon, a 32-pdr rifled gun, and a 32-pdr smoothbore gun. Guns facing the neck included two 12-pdr howitzers, two 8in shell guns, three 32-pdr carronades, two 32-pdr howitzers, one 42-pdr carronade, and one 10in seacoast mortar; these last two were not in embrasures.

Battery Wagner's moat was designed to be flooded at high tide. At the bottom of the moat was a palisade wall and embedded in Battery Wagner's face were pikes that faced an attacker. To protect the garrison, a bombproof measuring 31×130ft was capable of sheltering 900 standing men; there was also a wooden barracks building and an officers' quarters within the fort. Wells were sunk within the fort. About 250yd from Battery Wagner was a slight sand ridge where the Confederates dug rifle pits. Between Battery Wagner and the rifle pits "torpedoes," as landmines were then called, were planted.

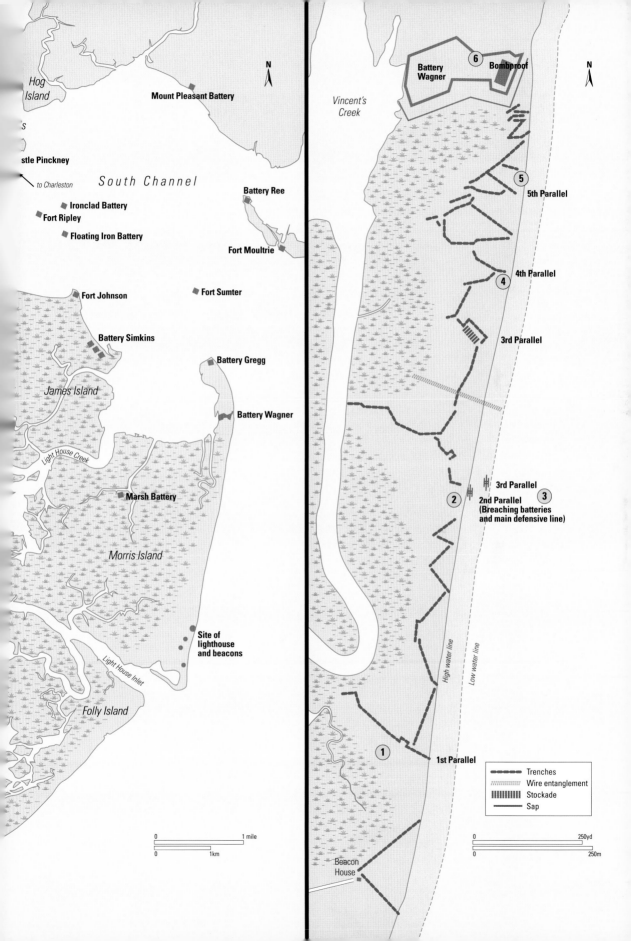

Left map:

Hog
Island

Mount Pleasant Battery

N

s

stle Pinckney

to Charleston

South Channel

Battery Ree

Ironclad Battery

Fort Ripley

Floating Iron Battery

Fort Moultrie

Fort Johnson

Fort Sumter

Battery Simkins

Battery Gregg

James Island

Battery Wagner

Light House Creek

Marsh Battery

Morris Island

Site of
lighthouse
and beacons

Light House Inlet

Folly Island

0   1 mile

0   1km

Right map:

Battery
Wagner   ⑥   Bombproof

Vincent's
Creek

N

⑤

5th Parallel

4th Parallel

④

3rd Parallel

3rd Parallel

⑨②

2nd Parallel
(Breaching batteries
and main defensive line)

③

High water line

Low water line

①

1st Parallel

Trenches

Wire entanglement

Stockade

Sap

Beacon
House

0   250yd

0   250m

INTO COMBAT

The besiegers maintained a constant bombardment during the day, but damage to Battery Wagner was minimal as its quartz-crystal sand had no cohesive property. At night, work parties need only throw the sand back into place to repair the position. Knowing that Battery Wagner was under siege, on July 21 the position's commander, Brigadier General Johnson Hagood, made a request for sharpshooters equipped with Whitworth rifles: "Please send me a few Whitworth rifles; these sharpshooters have them, and annoy me very much" (OR, Series I, Vol. XXVIII, Part 1: 430). (To minimize combat fatigue, the garrison and its commander were regularly rotated off at night.) According to Hagood, the Confederate strategy for defending Battery Wagner involved the active use of sharpshooters in concert with limited artillery at Battery Wagner, alongside artillery support from farther afield; the battery's garrison was to make full use of the bombproof so they could repel any Union assault (Hagood 1997: 182). At first the ordinary infantry, armed with Enfields, undertook sharpshooting duties. Later, at Hagood's suggestion, a small sharpshooting unit was created from picked men of the 21st and 27th South Carolina Infantry; they were commanded by W.D. Woodbery of Charleston's Washington Light Infantry and equipped with the Whitworth rifle, small numbers of which had evaded the Union blockade. Woodbery's men were posted to Sullivan's Island to undertake a few days' target practice before commencing duty at Battery Wagner (Hagood 1997: 184). The consignment sent to Charleston was made up of 13 rifles.

While W.D. Woodbery's sharpshooters were training, Gillmore's engineers worked day and night and finished the first parallel on July 23. The parallel included eight siege and field guns, ten mortars, and five Billinghurst Requa Battery guns. Assisting in the siege were six Union sharpshooters, one of whom was Private Edgar King of the 7th Connecticut Volunteer Infantry. According to King, the Billinghurst guns and the six sharpshooters were encamped on the western side of the island; each evening, the sharpshooters prepared bullets and patches for their scoped target rifles (Tourtellotte 1988: 173–74).

The next day, July 24, Union artillery chief Colonel John W. Turner delivered more artillery to Morris Island. From Turner we learn the threat posed to the besiegers by Woodbery's Whitworth-armed sharpshooters:

> Where we landed our artillery on Morris Island to our batteries was a distance varying from 1½ to 2 miles. This entire distance was heavy sand, through which all the guns were dragged into position by troops at night. Seven heavy guns were thus dragged to the immediate front of Fort Wagner, put into position, equipped, magazines filled, and the batteries served for seven days, though within half range of seven heavy pieces of artillery with which that place was garnished and within 400 yards of their sharpshooters, with their whole front covered with marksmen armed with telescopic rifles of extraordinary power. (OR, Series I, Vol. XXVIII, Part 1: 214)

In his journal entry for July 25, Captain Louis F. Emilio of the 54th Massachusetts reported the Confederate sharpshooters' arrival, and noted their harassment of the Union working parties on Morris Island (Emilio 1969: 108). Also noticing their effect was the Union's chief engineer, Major Thomas B. Brooks:

Continued work in second parallel day and night, strengthening parapets of approaches, revetting breast heights, building splinter proof shelters, and constructing breaching battery. Only a small detachment of engineers work during the day, the heavy work being all done at night. This arrangement is made necessary by the enemy's sharpshooters, who during this period give us more trouble by day than his heavy guns. The least exposure above the crest of the parapet will draw the fire of his telescopic Whitworths, which cannot be dodged. Several of our men were wounded by these rifles at a distance of 1,300 yards from Wagner, where prisoners informed us the riflemen were stationed. (OR, Series I, Vol. XXVIII, Part 1: 277)

Included among the casualties on the second parallel were the artillerymen of Battery Meade and Battery Rose who exposed themselves to aim their pieces or to observe the fall of their shot.

Unlike sharpshooters in other armies, Battery Wagner's Whitworth sharpshooters were excused from all camp and night duty. Confederate ordnance officer Captain Samuel A. Ashe described one pair's tactics (Morrow 1989: 101). Having made a pair of loopholes by removing sandbags, Ashe's sharpshooters stood ready; raising a hat on a ramrod attracted the attention of their Union opposite number, who would expose himself while trying to get a better look, prompting the Whitworth-armed sharpshooters to open fire.

The growing Union casualties could not be ignored and in his report for July 23–24, Gillmore reported: "There has been no fighting since the 18th, except engagements between the sharpshooters on both sides, and daily but desultory bombardments... I lose 3 or 4 men daily ..." (OR, Series I, Vol. XXVIII, Part 1: 203). To protect Gillmore's artillerists, rope mantlets were attached to the guns, but while the mantlets could defeat a Minié ball, they could not stop a Whitworth bolt. Boilerplate mantlets were fabricated and installed in the embrasures in their place, but by the time they were emplaced, the Whitworth sharpshooters had switched to concentrate on the engineers. Their superiority convinced Major Brooks that the Union pickets were not up to the task of acting as sharpshooters. Better men were needed.

Acting on Brooks' suggestion, Brigadier General Alfred H. Terry, the commander of the 1st Division, made arrangements on August 2 for testing all the men in his brigade. The top 50 or 60 would be formed into a special ad hoc sharpshooter company led by Captain Richard Ela, 3d New Hampshire, and Lieutenant A.H.C. Jewett, 4th New Hampshire. The men would be placed in a separate camp and issued Springfield rifles – the best that could be had at the time. It took several days to select the men and then to train them. In the meantime, the Confederate sharpshooters continued to annoy any unwary Union soldier. Twice on August 6 they managed to cut the telegraph line connecting the Union trenches to the headquarters, far to the rear. The second parallel was completed on August 9 and the third parallel begun 540yd away from Battery Wagner. The third parallel would contain loopholes for the Union sharpshooters.

In the early-morning hours of August 10, Woodbery's men were relieved by 20 men led by Lieutenant John E. Dugger, 8th North Carolina Infantry. (The two groups would relieve each other for the remainder of the siege.) The freshness of Dugger's men became immediately apparent to Brooks, who wrote, "The fire of the enemy's sharpshooters was particularly brisk during

Battery Rosecrans was built on the western end of the second parallel and was 830yd from Battery Wagner, 2,100yd from Battery Gregg, and 3,500yd from Fort Sumter. Weighing 9,727lb each, Battery Rosecrans' three 6.4in 100-pdr Parrott rifles were of cast-iron construction and featured a reinforcing wrought-iron band. When loaded with a 10lb charge of powder each piece could hurl a shell 6,900yd and with a 30-degree elevation, even farther, to 7,810yd. To protect the Parrott rifles and their crews from fire from Confederate artillery or Whitworth-armed sharpshooters, Battery Rosecrans was fitted with metal embrasures. (Buyenlarge/Getty Images)

the day" (OR, Series I, Vol. XXVIII, Part 1: 285). Their deadly fire was noted by Private King, who witnessed the death of a comrade hit by a Confederate bullet as he observed the fall of a mortar shell (Tourtellotte 1988: 172).

Three days later, on August 13, Ela's special detachment of sharpshooters entered the trenches. While their Springfield rifle-muskets were inferior to the Whitworth, as the distance between the two sides closed, the advantage started shifting to the Union. For one thing, since the Springfield fouled less than the Whitworth, its rate of fire was higher. Lieutenant Henry Little described the Union sharpshooters' tactics:

Each man was required to carry his rations for the day, and one hundred rounds of ammunition, and generally disposed of both rations and cartridges before returning to camp. These sharpshooters were stationed in the advance trenches, and it was their duty, so far as possible, to keep the enemy's sharpshooters quiet, and silence the guns in Fort Wagner. To do this was a very dangerous task and required the utmost vigilance. It was almost sure death for a man to show his head above the breastworks, and extra protection was obtained by piling up coarse gunny bags filled with sand. Loop-holes were obtained at proper intervals by leaving the ends of the lower bags about two inches apart and then filling up with sand so as to leave the hole about three inches high. It was not safe to watch through these holes, and precautions had to be taken to get into "position," as "darkening" the loop-hole was sure to draw the fire of the ever watchful "reb," unless he thought our men were fooling him. The rifles were first placed through

the loop-holes at arm's length and then a cap was placed above the rifle to prevent the "reb" sharpshooter from seeing through. This would generally draw his fire, and at the same time some of our men were closely watching for his fire from the other loop-holes, in order to send a shot back while there was a prospect of hitting someone. It required considerable study to draw the fire of the enemy and at the same time make it harmless for our men. One of the expedients was to place a cap on a ramrod and raise it about an inch above the works over the loop-hole. If it were raised higher, they knew it was a deception and would not fire at it. Another way was to place a cap alternatively before the loop-hole and then remove it, in order to make them think it was a man. (Little 1896: 163–64)

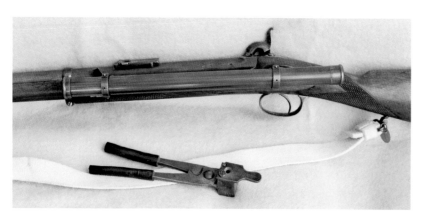

This Whitworth rifle has a side-mounted Davidson scope; the bullet mold is lying atop the sling. Weighing little more than a rifle-musket, the Whitworth was the ideal longarm for sniping. A sharpshooter armed with a Whitworth was very mobile, and could hit man-sized targets at ranges in excess of 1,000yd. Developed by the British engineer Sir Joseph Whitworth, the .451-caliber Whitworth rifle had a hexagonal bore with a 1:20in twist. It fired a mechanically fitted bullet that was made to tighter tolerances that fitted the bore. This, along with fouling, made the Whitworth slower to load. While capable of hitting a 32ft×2ft target at 1,800yd, the Whitworth's slower rate of fire made it unsuitable for skirmishing, but very well adapted for precision sharpshooting. (Martin Pegler)

Duel on Morris Island

Confederate view: While some Whitworth sharpshooters are fighting from loopholes they built in Battery Wagner, these two, along with a company of infantry, are fighting from the rifle pits 200yd from Battery Wagner. One sharpshooter has just fired while another is reloading. The shallowness of the rifle pit compels him to roll onto his back to avoid exposure while reloading. The scarcity of British-made Whitworth accessories resulted in improvisations such as the use of standard cartridge boxes without the tins to allow for the longer Whitworth cartridge.

Up to now they have been unchallenged and have shot through rope merlons to inflict casualties among the Union artillerymen. Several times they cut the telegraph wire running between the sap and headquarters in the rear. At times harassment by the Whitworth sharpshooters prevents any progress by the sappers and the slightest exposure by any Union soldier invites a Whitworth bolt. In response to their effectiveness, intense bombardments have driven most Confederates into the confined and stifling environment of Wagner's bombproof, leaving only a handful of men like those in the rifle pits to fight. During those desperate moments when Wagner's artillery was silenced, the only return fire against the Union forces is from the sharpshooters.

Union view: Joining the siege batteries and the guns of the blockading squadron on August 13, the long-awaited soldiers of Captain Richard Ela's 60-man corps of select sharpshooters drawn from numerous regiments help to suppress the Confederate sharpshooters who have been impeding the progress of the sap. Divided into two platoons, one fights one day under Captain Ela and the other the next day under Lieutenant A.H.C. Jewett. The rotation allows the men to relax for a day away from battle. Like their Confederate counterparts, they leave their quarters before dawn and carry with them enough water, rations, and 100 cartridges for the day. They remain there all day, returning only after dark. Cat-like patience, observation skills, steady marksmanship, and cunning are required by the men in this life-and-death struggle.

Loopholes are plugged with kepis or anything else to keep the Confederates from guessing which loophole is being used. One sharpshooter helps his partner by raising his kepi above the sandbags to entice a Confederate to shoot. His partner lies in wait with his finger on the trigger, waiting for the smoke from a Whitworth to reveal a Confederate sharpshooter's presence.

On August 18, a storm flooded the third parallel and washed away portions of the second parallel. Repair work commenced immediately and anyone careless enough to expose himself was shot. One Union artilleryman was shot in the head and killed and two others were wounded. The repairs to the two parallels were complete the following day. Battery Wagner came under heavy bombardment, which silenced its artillery. The Whitworth-armed sharpshooters fired back and even turned their guns against the Union Navy monitors that bombarded them. Under cover of the heavy artillery fire, the Union engineers dug another 100yd to extend the third parallel. The third parallel was completed on August 21 and work on a fourth parallel began immediately. About this time, the lines were so close that the Union besiegers realized that among the Confederate sharpshooters was an African American. Lieutenant A.H.C Jewett described how one of his men, perhaps still a teenager, was shot and killed while trying to catch a glimpse of the African-American sharpshooter through a port hole (Jewett 1944: 38–41). In Jewett's view, this particular sharpshooter was especially to be feared, as he seemed to be armed with a large-caliber sporting rifle that was highly accurate at long range. Brigadier General George H. Gordon, commanding the Union troops on Folly Island, also complained about the African-American sharpshooter (Gordon 1882: 194).

On August 26, the extension to the third parallel allowed one regiment, the 24th Massachusetts Volunteer Infantry, to storm the rifle pits in front of Battery Wagner. Surprised, the Confederate forces fired one volley and were unwilling to retreat through a minefield; 61 men were captured and only a handful of Confederates escaped. Corporal James H. Gooding, 54th Massachusetts, described how of 63 prisoners, five were African Americans, with two of these five being equipped as sharpshooters (Adams 1991: 53–54).

The seized rifle pits were incorporated into a fifth parallel and the Confederate sharpshooters now had to fight within the confines of Battery Wagner. Parrott rifles were bore-sighted at the sandbags that protected the Confederate sharpshooters. Any time a sharpshooter fired, a Parrott rifle that was trained on his position responded. If nothing else, such activity destroyed the sandbags and demoralized the Confederate sharpshooters. As a precautionary measure, double-barrel shotguns were also issued to the Confederate sharpshooters; at such close proximity, to prevent their capture most of the Whitworths had already been withdrawn from service and replaced with Enfield rifles, which offered comparable accuracy at closer ranges and could be loaded faster than a Whitworth, and which were superior in range to the Springfield.

Approaching a loophole became a dangerous affair for the Confederates. Major John G. Pressley, 25th South Carolina Infantry, describes how they adapted:

> The men of the Twenty-fifth were in high spirits, a great many of them went to work building defences [*sic*] with sand bags on the walls of the fort. They constructed loop-holes in these defences, through which to shoot at the enemy, whose works were provided with similar means of offense and defense. Firing from these loopholes had become very dangerous, yet it was steadily kept up. As soon as light was seen through one of these holes the Federal sharpshooter fired, and not infrequently succeed in sending their balls through. Each side fired at the flashes

On September 7, 1863, in the predawn hours before the final assault on Battery Wagner, Captain Richard Ela's sharpshooters were ordered to approach Battery Wagner under the cover of darkness. Half of them, as shown here, deployed to the rifle pits in front of the fifth parallel with the remainder in the zigzag approaches from the fifth parallel. They were instructed to suppress Confederate gunners in the embrasures and provide cover for their comrades who would storm Battery Wagner. Luckily for both sides, the Confederates in Battery Wagner were busy evacuating it, as the defense of the position had become untenable and the garrison could be more useful elsewhere. (Buyenlarge/Getty Images)

of the rifle of the other. Our men, after firing, shoved their hats into the loop-holes to darken them before they drew out their muskets, which, when reloaded, were put carefully back into the hole covered by the man before the hat was withdrawn. One man, Private Wallace, of Company C, received a ball in his piece, which, happening to be of larger caliber than the enemy's gun, did not lodge. He took it out, put down a charge of powder and set the ball back to its former owner. Musketry firing and hissing of balls were incessant. (Pressley 1888: 158)

Thanks to heavy suppressive fire, Union engineers reached Battery Wagner's protective ditch on September 6. Through hard work they had finally gained the upper hand and preparations were made to storm Battery Wagner. Realizing Battery Wagner was lost, the Confederates began to evacuate Morris Island at 2300hrs on September 6. One Confederate deserter waded ashore and reported the evacuation. Threatened with death if he was lying, he swore that the Confederates were gone. Terry sent a probing patrol, which approached cautiously. They found Battery Wagner had been abandoned and mined, but that the fuze had extinguished itself. Joyously they rushed to Cumming's Point in time to capture the last boatload of departing Confederates. Among the prisoners captured were several slaves. Jewett described their predicament when they were marched back to Battery Wagner, noting that they were set upon by enraged Union soldiers who believed that one of them might be the African-American sharpshooter who had inspired such fear during the fighting (Jewett 1944: 41). After a 49-day siege, Morris Island was finally under Union control.

A poorly coordinated amphibious landing to capture Fort Sumter on September 8 failed. The Confederates read the signals between Gillmore and Rear Admiral John A. Dahlgren, Gillmore's naval counterpart, and prepared a warm reception for the landings. They easily repelled the initial landing; seeing its failure, the Army landing force turned back. Unable to capture Fort Sumter, Gillmore asked the Union Navy blockading squadron to sail past Fort Sumter and bombard Charleston into submission. Fearing Confederate torpedoes, Dahlgren demurred and contented himself with bombarding Fort Sumter and its surrounding forts. Instead of seeking another approach, Gillmore became myopic and steadfastly stuck to his plan. Charleston would not be captured until February 18, 1865 when Gillmore, having returned from his Virginia interlude, landed north of Charleston at Bull's Bay. With Major General William T. Sherman's army marching up from the south, the Confederates abandoned Charleston.

Analysis

FREDERICKSBURG

At Fredericksburg, Captain William Plumer's 1st Andrew Sharpshooters along with skirmishers from two volunteer infantry regiments, the 7th Michigan and 19th Massachusetts, fought against the hidden Confederate sharpshooters who had driven away the engineers who were attempting to bridge the Rappahannock River. Brigaded with Plumer's company was Captain William F. Russell's 2d Minnesota Sharpshooters Company; it is not clear why they were not ordered to join the 1st Andrew Sharpshooters. Other sharpshooter units, including Berdan's two regiments, belonged to different Union corps not involved in the river crossing. This lack of numbers among the Union sharpshooters deployed during the bridging operation hampered the Union effort to cross the Rappahannock.

A second problem facing the 1st Andrew Sharpshooters at Fredericksburg was that the men of that company were compelled to shoot at the smoke signatures from the Confederates' rifles. This can be effective against an individual sharpshooter, but when the enemy's positions were masked by the smoke signatures from the fire of hundreds of other Confederates as well as all the Union shells that were fired during the bombardment, it was a daunting task which they were incapable of mastering. Additionally, Burnside's decision to mass his artillery into a "grand battery" failed to break the Confederate resistance.

Across the Rappahannock, the handful of Confederate sharpshooters took full advantage of fighting defensively from entrenched positions or from Fredericksburg's houses. They successfully contested the bridge-building efforts until Union infantry forces performed an amphibious assault and secured the waterfront by driving the sharpshooters away. While the Confederate sharpshooters could not and did not win the battle for the Confederacy, they delayed completion of the bridges, which gained time for Jackson's Corps

Vicksburg, 1863: Union trenches around the 3d Louisiana Redan after it was blown. In the foreground is a trench used to feed Union soldiers into the fight. Atop of it is a gabion-lined wall with loopholes used by Union sharpshooters. Rising in the center background is "Coonskin's Tower," from which Union troops could shoot exposed Confederates and study the enemy lines. Lieutenant Henry C. "Coonskin" Foster placed mirrors on the tower to assist mortarmen in shelling the Confederates. The Confederates shot out the mirrors, but Foster replaced them regularly. (Library of Congress)

to join Lee and secure his right flank. Viewed from that perspective, the sharpshooters made the Confederate victory possible at Fredericksburg, for if Burnside could have crossed before Jackson's arrival, the Union general could have flanked Lee and driven him away before turning on Jackson.

VICKSBURG

Owing to both sides' shortage of sharpshooters during the siege of Vicksburg, marksmen from infantry regiments were called upon to fight as sharpshooters. Easily the most distinguished figure among the Union soldiers was Lieutenant Henry C. "Coonskin" Foster, who was given command of a 100-strong ad hoc sharpshooter unit. While the besiegers revived the American Revolutionary War practice of building a Maham-style log tower that dominated the Confederate position, the Union forces also made a number of innovations – including an early form of the periscope, the periscope rifle, and burrowing into the ground for a sniping post.

While the handful of Confederate sharpshooters initially held the upper hand at Fredericksburg, the Confederate sharpshooters at Vicksburg were hard pressed by their Union besiegers who were much more innovative in their siege works and fieldcraft as well as being supported by the superior Union artillery. The Union besiegers eventually prevailed, partially because the Confederates had entrenched along the ridge where they were silhouetted against the skyline instead of digging farther down the hill to reduce their exposure. Eventually, the Confederate sharpshooters along with the rest of the Confederate garrison were starved into submission.

BATTERY WAGNER

During the siege of Battery Wagner, the sole battalion of Confederate sharpshooters, the 1st Battalion South Carolina Sharpshooters, did not

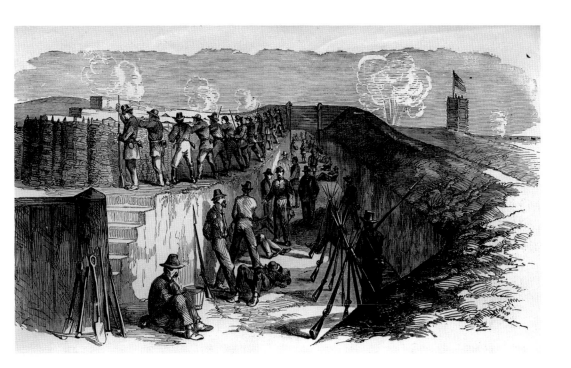

serve on Morris Island. They were sharpshooters in name only, and fought as line infantry. Instead, the Confederates relied on two small ad hoc units that received familiarization with the highly desirable Whitworth rifle. Their effectiveness hampered the Union siege operations and compelled the besiegers to raise their own sharpshooter company, commanded by Captain Richard Ela. Ela's men honed their marksmanship, but were armed with the inferior Springfield rifle-musket. While the Confederates held the upper hand at longer ranges, they lost their ballistic advantage of more accurate long-range fire when the Union lines closed the distance. In fact, considering the Whitworth's lower rate of fire, it became less desirable to have such a valuable weapon within close proximity to the enemy – especially when the ordinary Enfield rifle-musket was accurate enough.

Upon cessation of the siege of Battery Wagner, the sharpshooters of both sides returned to their parent units and the Confederate Whitworth rifles were returned to storage. One or two Whitworth rifles did go to Fort Sumter and the sharpshooters there hit a couple of Union soldiers on Morris Island. However, the Whitworth sharpshooters could not change the course of the siege; they could only forestall the end, and the almost two-month-long siege of Battery Wagner allowed the Confederates to improve their defenses around Charleston Harbor. Even Morris Island's capture became moot, as Fort Sumter remained in Confederate hands and locked the Union out of Charleston Bay.

Gillmore became fixated on his plan, lost sight of his objective, and failed to develop a new strategy. It took a year and a half, which included some fighting in Virginia, before Gillmore landed a force north of Charleston's defenses at Bull's Bay and approached Charleston from its unguarded point in February 1865. By that time, however, it was clear that the Confederacy was almost finished and that Charleston had lost its significance as a prize.

Lieutenant Henry C. "Coonskin" Foster's sharpshooters are shown here firing from their loopholes at Vicksburg. Note the gabion walls that protect them from return fire. The uniformity of the loopholes suggests they were made of wood and not sandbags. Behind them is a trench which allowed men to move along the lines in relative safely and to relax when not fighting. It was not unknown for these trenches to be covered with boughs to provide shade from the oppressive sun. In the right background is "Coonskin's Tower," which provided an excellent observation post from which Union sharpshooters could harass the Confederates. (Buyenlarge/Getty Images)

Aftermath

With respect to marksmanship or skill, it cannot be concluded that either side was superior to the other during the Civil War. In the early battles up to 1862, the Union held the upper hand with more sharpshooters and superior guns that included both breechloaders and long-range target rifles. Unsuitable for skirmishing, most target rifles were sent home and the remaining few were kept in the regimental wagon for use when needed. By 1863, the Confederates were fielding more sharpshooter battalions, many of which were equipped with the British Enfield rifle. Additionally, a few select Confederates were issued the long-range Whitworth and Kerr rifles that were slipping past the blockade. It has been estimated that upward of 250 of the Whitworths reached the Confederacy.

In early 1864, sharpshooting was finally fully implemented within General Robert E. Lee's Army of Northern Virginia. Lee did not press the issue until early in 1864, after Major General Cadmus M. Wilcox suggested that each brigade raise its own sharpshooter battalion – almost two years after Adjutant General Samuel Cooper had issued the order. Lee needed a tactical edge to give his battered army an advantage in the face of the growing numerical superiority of his enemy. Moreover, Brigadier General Johnson Hagood's experiences at Battery Wagner and Petersburg (May 6–December 20, 1864) led Hagood to conclude that there should be at least one scoped rifle-armed sharpshooter per regiment.

The effectiveness of Lee's sharpshooter battalions compelled numerous elements of the Army of the Potomac to raise their own ad hoc battalions. By 1864, however, the early Union sharpshooter units in the Army of the Potomac were severely depleted by attrition. Attempts to replenish their ranks proved difficult because recruiters vied with recruiters from existing and new units. In the end, some Union divisions or brigades resorted to raising their own ad hoc sharpshooting battalions. Fortunately for these units, their officers were experienced veterans who understood the distinction between the two types of sharpshooters as well as how best to use them.

Distinguishing between the sharpshooter who was a skirmisher and the sharpshooter who was a sniper, Major General Frank Wheaton, commanding 1st Division, VI Corps, used the former as expert skirmishers and withheld the latter to support his attack with their target guns at the Third Battle of Petersburg on April 2, 1865. This was demonstrated during his attack on Brigadier General James H. Lane's Brigade of North Carolinians when Wheaton's Spencer-armed sharpshooters went forward as skirmishers, their rapid-firing repeaters forcing the Confederates down. Supporting them were Wheaton's target rifle-armed sharpshooters who provided covering fire. Only after the Confederate works were carried did the target rifle-armed sharpshooters move forward to engage the Confederates at Fort Welch.

Similarly, the remaining members of Berdan's Sharpshooters found that if they had target rifles, they could avoid close-quarter combat. They fought at the Wilderness (May 5–7, 1864), Spotsylvania Court House (May 9, 1864), the North Anna (May 23–26, 1864), Second Cold Harbor (May 31–June 12, 1864), and the siege of Petersburg (June 9, 1864–March 25, 1865). It had taken over three years of war before Berdan's vision of sharpshooting was finally recognized in the Union Army. This was, of course, too late for Berdan, who had resigned on January 2, 1864, and for many of his men who had been killed, wounded, discharged for medical reasons, or whose term of enlistment neared expiration.

While sharpshooting became an integral part of the Civil War battlefield, the tactics and techniques refined during the war had no place in the postwar US Army. No sharpshooting manual or treatise was written or doctrine adopted, and everything learned from the war was forgotten as Americans set aside their differences and wrestled with the challenges of rebuilding (in the case of the South) or looked toward westward expansion. Marksmanship, though, was acknowledged as necessary. The appallingly poor marksmanship exhibited during the Civil War was addressed by the postwar Army through marksmanship competitions with medals and monthly bonuses for the winners. Additionally, former officers, including Ambrose Burnside, created the (American) National Rifle Association or NRA to promote marksmanship and rifle practice. One NRA officer, G.W. Wingate, wrote the popular *Manual for Rifle Practice* (1872), while Colonel T.T.S. Laidley's *A Course of Instruction in Rifle Firing* (1879) was approved by the Army. Both were superseded in 1885 by Captain S.E. Blunt's *Instructions for Rifle and Carbine Firing in the United States Army.*

The most widely issued lever-action rifle, the .56-56 Spencer was fed through a seven-shot magazine located in the stock. The magazine plate was swiveled out of the way and seven cartridges could be dropped into the magazine tube, which was better protected from the elements than the Henry's open-bottomed magazine. To use the Spencer, the hammer was manually cocked and the lever then worked to feed a cartridge from the magazine. The Spencer was made in both a short- and a long-barrel infantry version. It was harder-hitting than the Henry and was issued to the 5th, 6th, 7th, and 8th companies of Ohio Sharpshooters. (USNPS Photo, Springfield Armory National Historic Site, SPAR 4870)

SELECT BIBLIOGRAPHY

Abernethy, Byron R., ed. (1958). *Private Elisha Stockwell Jr., Sees the Civil War.* Norman, OK: University of Oklahoma Press.

Adams, J.G.B. (1899). *Reminiscences of the Nineteenth Massachusetts Regiment.* Boston, MA: Wright & Potter Printing Co.

Alexander, Edward Porter (1990). *Military Memoirs of a Confederate.* Dayton, OH: Morningside Press.

Ames, John W. (1995). "In Front of the Stone Wall at Fredericksburg," in *Battles and Leaders*, Vol. III, Part I. Edison, NJ: 122–25.

Ames, Nelson (2000). *History of Battery G, First Regiment New York Light Artillery.* Wolcott, NY: Benedum Books.

Anonymous (1864). "Colonel Berdan," in *The Portrait Monthly* Vol. 2, No. 18 (December 1864): 85.

Aschmann, Rudolf (1972). *Memoirs of a Swiss Officer in the American Civil War.* Bern: Herbert Lang.

Barker, Lorenzo (1994). *With the Western Sharpshooters.* Huntington, AL: Blue Acorn.

Bearss, Edwin Cole (1986). *The Vicksburg Campaign,* Vol. III. Dayton, OH: Morningside Press.

Bearss, Edwin Cole, ed. (1998). *A Southern Record: The Story of the 3d Louisiana Infantry, C.S.A.* Dayton, OH: Morningside Books.

Bell, John S. (1904). "Arkansas Sharpshooters at Vicksburg," in *Confederate Veteran Magazine,* Vol. XII, 1904: 446–47.

Benham, Calhoun (1863). *A System for Conducting Musketry Instruction.* Richmond, VA: Prepared and printed by order of General Bragg for the Army of Tennessee.

Bennett, Stewart & Barbara Tillery (2004). *The Struggle for the Life of the Republic: A Civil War Narrative by Brevet Major Charles Dana Miller, 76th Ohio Volunteer Infantry.* Kent, OH: Kent State University Press.

Benson, Susan, ed. (1992). *Confederate Scout-Sharpshooter: The Civil War Memoirs of Berry Benson.* Athens, GA: University of Georgia Press.

Bilby, Joseph G. (1996). *Civil War Firearms.* New York, NY: Da Capo Press.

Brown, Russell K. (2004). *Our Connection with Savannah: A History of the 1st Battalion Georgia Sharpshooters.* Macon, GA: Mercer University Press.

Buck, Irving (1985). *Cleburne and His Command.* Dayton, OH: Morningside Press.

Burt, Richard W. (1863). Letter to the *Newark True American.* May 30, 1863. Vicksburg National Military Park.

Cleveland, H.W.S. (1864). *Hints to Riflemen.* New York, NY: D. Appleton & Co.

Coffin, Charles Carleton (1887). *My Days and Nights on the Battlefield.* Boston, MA: Dana Estes & Co.

Crumb, Herb S. & Katherine Dhalle, eds (1993). *No Middle Ground: Thomas Ward Osborn's Letters From the Field.* Hamilton, NY: Edmonston.

Dalton, Peter, ed. (2002). *Soldiers in Green.* Sandy Point, ME: Richardson's Civil War Round Table.

Davis, E. Elden, ed. (2007). *"the boys call them … 'Sharpfellers'" Letters from Company C, 1st Regiment Berdan's United States Sharp Shooters.* Howell, MI: E. Elden Davis.

Davis, William Little (1862). Letter of Dec. 16, 1862, Catalog #Z27f. Mississippi Department of Archives and History.

Dickinson, Jack L., ed. (1997). *Diary of a Confederate Sharpshooter: The Life of James Conrad Peters.* Charleston, SC: Pictorial History.

Dunlop, William S. (1899). *Lee's Sharpshooters or The Forefront of Battle,* Dayton, OH: Morningside Press.

Eddington, William R. (n.d.). "My Civil War Memoirs." Available at: https://macoupin.illinoisgenweb.org/military/civilwar/eddingtonwilliamr.html

Emilio, Louis F. (1969). *A Brave Black Regiment.* New York, NY: Arno Press & New York Times.

Gallagher, Gary W., ed. (1989). *Fighting for the Confederacy.* Chapel Hill, NC: University of North Carolina Press.

Gordon, George H. (1882). *A War Diary of Events in the War of the Great Rebellion, 1863–65.* Boston, MA: James R. Osgood & Co.

Grant, U.S. (1885). *Personal Memoirs*, Vol. 1. New York, NY: Charles L. Webster & Co.

Hagood, Johnson (1997). *Memoirs of the War of Secession.* Camden, SC: J. Fox Reprints.

Hardee, William J. (1861). *Rifle and Light Infantry Tactics; For the Exercise and Manoeuvres of Troops When Acting as Light Infantry Or Riflemen*, Vol I. Philadelphia, PA: J.B. Lippincott & Co.

Hennessy, John, ed. (2000). *Fighting with the Eighteenth Massachusetts: The Civil War Memoirs of Thomas H. Mann.* Baton Rouge, LA: Louisiana State University Press.

Herek, Raymond J. (1998). *These Men Have Seen Hard Service: The First Michigan Sharpshooters in the Civil War*. Detroit, MI: Great Lake Books.

Heth, Henry (1858). *A System of Target Practice For the Use of Troops When Armed with the Musket, Rifle-Musket, Rifle, or Carbine*. Philadelphia, PA: Henry Carey Baird.

Hickenlooper, Andrew (1995). "The Vicksburg Mine," in *Battles and Leaders*, Vol. III, Part II. Edison, NJ: Castle: 539–42.

Hitchcock, George A. (1997). *From Ashby to Andersonville*. Cupertino, CA: Savas.

Jewett, A.H.C. (1944). *A Boy Goes to War*. Bloomington, IL: Grace J. Austin.

Johnson, John (1970). *The Defense of Charleston Harbor, 1861–1865*. Freeport, NY: Books for Libraries Press.

Jones, Samuel (no date). *The Siege of Charleston*. Salem, MA: Higginson Books.

Koonce, Donald B, ed. (2000). *Doctor to the Front: The Reflections of Confederate Surgeon Thomas Fanning Wood*. Knoxville, TN: University of Tennessee Press.

Little, Henry F.W. (1896). *The Seventh Regiment New Hampshire Volunteers in the War of the Rebellion*. Concord, NH: Ira C. Evans.

Logsdon, David R. (1999). *Eyewitnesses at the Battle of Fort Donelson*. Nashville, TN: Kettle Hills Press.

Longstreet, James (1992). *From Manassas to Appomattox*. New York, NY: Konechy & Konechy.

McCrea, Henry Vaughan (1992). *Red Dirt and Isinglass: A Wartime Biography of a Confederate Soldier*. Self-published.

McLaws, Lafayette (1995). "The Confederate Left at Fredericksburg," in *Battles and Leaders*, Vol. III, Part I. Edison, NJ: Castle: 86–94.

Miller, Richard E. & R.E. Mooney, eds (1994). *The Civil War: The Nantucket Experience Including the Memoirs of Josiah Fitch Murphey*. Nantucket, MA: Wesco.

Montgomery, George (1997). *Georgia Sharpshooter*. Macon, GA: Mercer University Press.

Morrison, James L., ed. (1975). *The Memoirs of Henry Heth*. Westport, CT: Greenwood Press.

Morrow, John A. (1989). *The Confederate Whitworth Sharpshooters*. Self-published.

Official Records of the Union and Confederate Armies in the War of the Rebellion (1902). Washington, DC: Government Printing Office.

Owen, William M. (1995). "A Hot Day on Marye's Heights," in *Battles and Leaders*, Vol. III, Part I. Edison, NJ: Castle: 97–99.

Palfrey, F.W. (2002). *Antietam and Fredericksburg*. Edison, NJ: Castle.

Patch, Eileen, ed. (2001). *This From George: The Civil War Letters of Sergeant George Magusta English, 1861–1865*. Binghamton, NY: Broome.

Pressley, John G. (1886). "Extracts from the Diary of Lieutenant-Colonel John G. Pressley, of the Twenty-fifth South Carolina Volunteers," in *Southern Historical Society Papers*, Vol. XIV, Jan–Dec. 1886: 35–62.

Pressley, John G. (1888). "The Wee Nee Volunteers of Williamsburg District, South Carolina, in the First (Hagood) Regiment," in *Southern Historical Society Papers*, Vol. XVI, Jan–Dec. 1888: 116–94.

Racine, Philip N. (1994). *Unspoiled Heart: The Journal of Charles Mattocks of the 17th Maine*. Knoxville, TN: University of Tennessee Press.

Ray, Fred S. (2006). *Shock Troops of the Confederacy: The Sharpshooter Battalions of the Army of Northern Virginia*. Asheville, NC: CFS Books.

Silliker, Ruth L. (1985). *The Rebel Yell & The Yankee Hurrah: The Civil War Journal of a Maine Volunteer*. Camden, ME: Down East Books.

Thompson, Ed Porter (1898). *History of the Orphan Brigade*. Louisville, KY: Lewis N. Thompson.

Tourtellotte, Jerome (1988). *A History of Company K of the Seventh Connecticut Volunteer Infantry in the Civil War*. Salem, MA: Higginson Books.

de Trobriand, Régis (1899). *Four Years With the Army of the Potomac*. Boston, MA: Ticknor & Co.

Turion, Kenneth, ed. (1994). *The Civil War Diary of J.E. Hodgkins*. Camden, ME: Picton Press.

Wheeler, Richard (1978). *The Siege of Vicksburg*. New York, NY: Thomas Crowell.

White, Russell C., ed. (1993). *The Civil War Diary of Wyman S. White*. Baltimore, MD: Butternut & Blue.

Wilcox, Cadmus (1859). *Rifles and Rifle Practices: An Elementary Treatise Upon the Theory of Rifle Firing, Explaining the Causes of Inaccuracy of Fire and the Manner of Correcting It*. New York, NY: Van Nostrand.

Winschel, Terrence (1999). *Triumph and Defeat*. Mason City, IA: Savas.

Wood, Anthony, ed. (no date). *Reminiscences of the 35th GA Regt. as Seen by a Sharpshooter at the Front*. Conyers, GA: THP Printing.

Yee, Gary (2017). *Sharpshooters: Marksmen Through the Ages*. Oxford: Casemate.

Young, John D. (1996). "A Campaign with Sharpshooters," in *Annals of the War*. Edison, NJ: Blue and Grey Press: 267–85.

INDEX

References to illustrations are shown in **bold**.

accoutrements **10**, **11**, **14**, **15**, 19, 26, **29**, **40–41**, **68–69**, 70
ad hoc sharpshooter bns/cos: (C) 16, 20, 32, 75; (U) 12, 65, 74, 76
African-American sharpshooters 22, 27–28, 60, 71, 72
Andrew Sharpshooters: 1st 8, 13, 18–19, 35, 38, **40–41**, 42, 46, 73; 2d 8, 19
Antietam/Sharpsburg 7, 16, 33, 34, 35, 46
Army of Northern Virginia 13–14, 15, 16, 17, 20, 26, 33, 76
Army of Tennessee 13, 15, 17, 22, 28
Army of the Potomac 9, 24–25, 33, 34, 38, 76
Army of the Tennessee **10**, **11**
artillery forces/pieces, targeting of 24, 30, 65: (C) 27, 28, 44, 46, 52, 53, 54, 70; (U) 28, 53, 62, 65, 70, 71, 73

Ball's Bluff 7, 35, 46
Barksdale, Brig. Gen. William 34, 36, 38, 42, 46, **46**
Barksdale's Mississippians 34, **39**, **45**, 46
Battery Wagner, siege of (1863) 7, 11, 22, 30, 59–62, **60–61**, **63**, 64–67, **68–69**, 70, 71–72, 76
use of sharpshooters 6: (C) 6, 22, 25, 62, 64–65, 65–66, **68–69**, 70, 71–72, 74–75; (U) 6, 60, 61, 62, 64, 65–66, 66–67, **68–69**, 70, 71–72, **72**, 75
Beauregard, Lt. Gen. Pierre G.T. 59, **65**
Bell, Capt. John S. 54–55, 56–57
Benham, Maj. Calhoun 13, 21
Berdan, Hiram **4**, 8, 9, 15, 24, 32, 73, 77
Berdan's Sharpshooters **4**, 8, 9, 15, 22, 24, 25, 26, 27, 77: 1st USSS 8, 12, 18, 23, 25, 32, 73; 2d USSS 8, 16, 18, 25, 28, 32, 73
Big Black River Ridge 48, 55
Birge, Col. John S. 9
Birge's Western Sharpshooters 9, 22, 26, 32
Blackford, Maj. Eugene 16, 26, 32
Blackford's sharpshooters 26
Brooks, Maj. Thomas B. 64–65, 65–66
bullet molds/sizers/starters 19, **29**, 25, 67
bullets 64, 67: Minié ball **4**, 5, 16, 26, **32**, 42, 53, 65
Burnside, Maj. Gen. Ambrose E. 33–34, 36, **37**, 38, 39, 44, 74, 73, 77

camouflage/concealment **6**, **10**, **11**, 25–28, 30, 34–35, 53, 55
cartridge boxes **11**, **14**, **68–69**, 70
Champion Hill (1863) **7**, 47–48, 55
Cleburne, Maj. Gen. Patrick R. 13, **13**, 24
Cleburne's Division 13, 28, 55
clothing/headgear **6**, **10**, **11**, **14**, **15**, 25–26, 27, **40–41**, 53, 54, 67, **68–69**, 70, 72
Colt Root Revolving Rifle 18, **18–19**, 23
Cooper, Adj. Gen. Samuel 13, 16, 20, 76
Couch, Maj. Gen. Darius N. 33, 35, **37**

Ela, Capt. Richard 30, 62, 65, 70, 72, 75
Ela's sharpshooters 30, 62, 65, 66, 70, **72**, 75
Enfield rifle-muskets 17, **16–17**, 25, 27, 75
Enfield rifles 14, 15, 15, 31, **30–31**, 71
use of (C) 31, 64, 71, 76 -
engineers, use of (U) 34, 36, **37**, 50, 52, 54, 56, 57–58, 61, 62, 64–65, 71, 72
targeting of 36, 38, 39, **40–41**, 42, 62, 65, 73

First Bull Run/Manassas 7, 34, 65
Foster, Lt. Henry C. "Coonskin" 50, 53, 54, 56, 74, 75
"Coonskin's" sharpshooters 56, 74, **75**
"Coonskin's Tower" 53, 54, **56**, 74, **75**
Fredericksburg, battle for 7, 16, 33–36, **34–35**, 37, 38–39, **39**, **40–41**, 42, 42–44, **45**, 46, 73
use of sharpshooters: (C) 34–35, 38, 39, **40–41**, 42, 46, 73–74; (U) 35, 38, 39, 42, **43**, 73

Gettysburg 7, 59
Gillmore, Brig. Gen. Quincy A. 59, 60, 61, 62, 64, **64**, 65, 72, 75
Grant, Maj. Gen. Ulysses S. 47–48, 53, 56, 64
battles for Vicksburg 6, 47–49, 50, **51**, 52, 55, 58
Green, Brig. Gen. Martin E. 50, 54, 56–57, 58, **58**

Hagood, Brig. Gen. Johnson 24, 59, 64, 76
Haines, Lt. Peter C. 54, 57–58
Hardee, Lt. Gen. William J. 20, 32, 64
Head, Truman ("California Joe") 12
Henry rifles 18, 22, **22**, 77
Heth, Maj. Gen. Henry 21, **21**
Howard, Brig. Gen. Oliver O. 35, 36, 44
hunting rifles, use of 11

Jackson, Lt. Gen. Thomas J. 34, 36, 44
Jackson's Corps 34, **37**, 73–74
Jewett, Lt. A.H.C. 65, 70, 71, 72

Kerr rifles 6, 13, 20, 76

Lee, General Robert E. 13, 16, 28, 33, 34, **37**, 44, 74, 76
Logan, Maj. Gen. John A. 48, 56, 57
Longstreet, Lt. Col. James 34, 42, 46
Longstreet's Corps 34, 36, **37**, 44

Malvern Hill 7, 12, 19, 46
McClellan, Maj. Gen. George B. **4**, 22–23, 33, 34
McGowan, Brig. Gen. Samuel 26
McGowan's Sharpshooters 15, 21, 32
McLaws, Maj. Gen. Lafayette 13, 36, **37**, 38, 42
McPherson, Maj. Gen. James B. 48, 50, 57, 58
Moon, Cpl. Edom T. 21, 27–28

Native American sharpshooters 25, 26, 27, 30–31

Palmetto Sharpshooters 22
paper-patch cutters 19, 25, 64
pellet primers 19
Pemberton, Lt. Gen. John C. 20, 47, 50, 52, 52, 53, 55, 58
periscope rifles 24, 74
Petersburg, siege of 7, 28, 76, 77
Pickett, Maj. Gen. George E. 15, 37
Plummer, Capt. William 35, 73
Porter, Rear Adm. David D. 6, 47, 53
Pressley, Lt. Col. John G. 20, 71–72

rifle pits, use of **68–69**, 70, 71, **72**

Saunders, Capt. John 18, 19, 35, 46
scopes 24, **25**, **29**, 59, 64, **67**, 76
Second Bull Run/Manassas 7, 16, 34, 35

Sedgwick, Maj. Gen. John 24, 46
Seven Days' Battles 16, 19, 34, 35
Sharps rifles **12**, 18, 19, **18–19**, 28
use of (U) 19, 35, **40–41**, 42
sharpshooter units, raising of 5, 8–9, 12, 13, 16, 17, 20–21, 32, 52, 65, 76
sharpshooter units (by State): AK 47, 54–55, 58; AL 13, 16, 32, 50; CT 59, 64; FL 36, **37**; GA 13, 21, 27–28; IL 9, 30, 48, 53, 54, 57; IN 53, 54, 57; KY 20; LA 50, 53; MA 19, 30, 31, 36, **37**, 39, 42, 43–44, 60, 64, 71, 73; ME 9, 26, 28, 32; MI 9, 22, 26, 27, 30, 36, **37**, 39, 42, 73; MN 73; MO 9, 55; MS 34, 36, **37**, 38, **39**, 43, **45**, 46; NC 13, 65; NH 65; NY 12, 26, 36, **37**, 39, 60; OH 9, 12, 52, 53, 77; PA 9, 36; SC 20, 64, 65, 71–72, 74–75; VA 21; WI 30, 31
Sherman, Maj. Gen. William T. 48, 54, 64, 72
Shiloh 7, 13, 53, 54, 65
shotguns, use of 71
sights 5, 6, **10**, 11, 14, 16, 19, 25, 26, **26**
skirmishers/skirmishing 5, 8, 12, 13, 16, 17–18, 20, 22, 23–24, **23**, 32, 35, 38, 42–43, 67, 73, 77
snipers, use of 5, 22, 24–25, 74, 77
Spencer rifles 9, 18, 77, 77
sporting guns/rifles 22, 71
Spotsylvania Court House 7, 24, 31, 77
Springfield rifle-muskets 5, 17, 26, 27, **26–27**, **30–31**, 64, 66
users: (C) 27, 53; (U) 9, 27, 30, 65, 66, 75
stalkers/stalking 28–31
Sumner, Maj. Gen. Edwin V. **33**, 38, 44, 46
Sykes, Brig. Gen. George 46

tactics 27–28, 53, 54, 65, 66
target rifles 12, 23, 24, 35
sharpshooter use 5, 25: (C) **6**; (U) 6, 10, **10**, **11**, 19, 23, 35, **40–41**, 42, 60, 64, 76, 77
sights/scopes for 11, 12, 17, 25, **25**, 28, **28**, **29**, 35
telescopic sights 6, 11, 12, 17, 25, **25**, 28, **28**, **29**, 35, 64, 65
Terry, Brig. Gen. Alfred H. 65, 72
training **4**, 9, **9**, 13, 17–19, 21–22, 65
distance estimation 5, 10, 14, **16**, 21
marksmanship manuals 13, 14, 17, 20, 21, 22, 32, 77
marksmanship schools 16, **16**, 21
Trepp, Col. Casper 8, 32
Trobriard, Brig. Gen. Régis de 24, 28

Union Navy 6, 47, 52, 53, 59, 60, 62, 70, 71, 72

Vicksburg, siege of (1863) 6, 7, 30, 47–48, **48**, 49, **49**, 50, 51, 52–58, 56, 57, 74
use of sharpshooters: (C) **14**, 15, 47, 52–53, 55, 57, 74; (U) 6, 10, **11**, 30, 52, 53–54, 55, 56–57, **57**, 58, **72**, 74, **74**, 75
Volcanic repeating arms 22

Whitworth rifles 6, 67, **67**, 76
use of (C) 6, 13, 20, 55, 62, 64, 65, 66, 67, **68–69**, 70, 71, 75, 76
Wilcox, Brig. Gen. Orlando B. 30, 33, **37**
Wilcox, Maj. Gen. Cadmus M. 21, 76

Yorktown, siege of 5, 6, 7, 22, 28, 35